Teaching P(
Social, Health and
Economic and
Relationships, (Sex)
and Health
Education in
Primary Schools

Teaching Personal, Social, Health and Economic and Relationships, (Sex) and Health Education in Primary Schools

Enhancing the Whole Curriculum

Edited by Victoria Pugh and Daniel Hughes

BLOOMSBURY ACADEMIC
LONDON • NEW YORK • OXFORD • NEW DELHI • SYDNEY

BLOOMSBURY ACADEMIC
Bloomsbury Publishing Plc
50 Bedford Square, London, WC1B 3DP, UK
1385 Broadway, New York, NY 10018, USA

BLOOMSBURY, BLOOMSBURY ACADEMIC and the Diana logo are trademarks
of Bloomsbury Publishing Plc

First published in Great Britain 2021

Cover design: Charlotte James
Cover image © Liderina/ Getty Images

A catalogue record for this book is available from the British Library.

Library of Congress Cataloging-in-Publication Data
Names: Pugh, Victoria (Lecturer in health education}, editor.
Title: Teaching personal, social, health and economic and relationships, (sex) and health education
in primary schools : enhancing the whole curriculum / edited by Victoria Pugh and Daniel Hughes.
Description: London ; New York : Bloomsbury Academic, 2021. | Includes bibliographical
references and index.
Identifiers: LCCN 2020035681 (print) | LCCN 2020035682 (ebook) | ISBN 9781350129887
(paperback) | ISBN 9781350129894 (hardback) | ISBN 9781350129917 (ebook) |
ISBN 9781350129900 (epub)
Subjects: LCSH: Health education (Elementary)—Great Britain.
Classification: LCC LB1588.G7 T43 2021 (print) | LCC LB1588.G7 (ebook) | DDC 372.370941—dc23
LC record available at https://lccn.loc.gov/2020035681
LC ebook record available at https://lccn.loc.gov/2020035682

ISBN: HB: 978-1-3501-2989-4
       PB: 978-1-3501-2988-7
       ePDF: 978-1-3501-2991-7
       eBook: 978-1-3501-2990-0

Typeset by RefineCatch Limited, Bungay, Suffolk
Printed and bound in Great Britain

To find out more about our authors and books visit www.bloomsbury.com
and sign up for our newsletters.

Contents

Introduction: PSHE and R(S)HE: Why Bother?
Victoria Pugh and Daniel Hughes 1

1 **We're All in this Together!** *Victoria Pugh* 11

2 **Controversial Issues in PSHE and R(S)HE**
Richard Woolley 23

3 **Little Learners in a Big World** *Lorna Williams* 33

4 **Picture-perfect Drama** *Sharon Lannie* 45

5 **Developing the 'E' in PSHE** *Ben Shakespeare* 57

6 **Super Science and the 'Health' in PSHE
and R(S)HE** *Elena Lengthorn and Rebecca
Saunders* 69

7 **There's More to RE** *Karen Bubb* 83

8 **Tackling PSHE and R(S)HE through PE**
Daniel Hughes 93

9 **'Being' and the Outdoors** *Daniel Hughes* 105

How to Use This Book

This book offers support to teachers, teaching assistants, support staff, student teachers and others involved in PSHE and R(S)HE education in the planning, delivery and assessment of a PSHE and R(S)HE curriculum. Its focus is to explore the ways in which PSHE and R(S)HE can be used to enhance a range of other curriculum subjects. There are opportunities throughout the chapters to engage with real-life case studies or examples from practice, reflection questions and considerations for settings. The areas covered within the book are by no means an exhaustive list but are used as interesting and thought-provoking examples which can enhance classroom practice and whole-school implementation.

Within each chapter

 Case Studies/Examples from Practice/Lesson Plans Each chapter includes two case studies, examples from practice or lesson plan examples which demonstrate possible scenarios which practitioners might face, and draw from examples across EYFS/KS1 and KS2. These form the basis of the discussion throughout the chapter.

 Reflections After each case study section there is an opportunity to reflect upon the scenario, providing a chance for you as the reader to think more deeply about the scenario, reflect upon your own practice or experience, and to begin to think about how this might impact upon your future practice.

 Points to Consider for Your Setting This feature encourages you to explore the conversation within your wider school community. These questions or ideas can be used as discussion starters in staff meetings, development meetings or governors' meetings. They offer ways to encourage whole-school approaches to the planning, delivery and assessment of PSHE and R(S)HE and to explore the issues and opportunities available to particular settings.

At the end of each chapter

Key Reading Listed here is key materials to enhance the chapter and your understanding of the discussions explored.

Further Reading Additional suggestions of useful resources are provided to help further develop understanding on specific topics.

We hope that by reading this book, you will gain the knowledge, skills and understanding of PSHE and R(S)HE curriculum design, implementation and development. As the reader, we would like to encourage you to reflect upon what these key issues mean to you as an educator and how they can be best applied within your own setting and what the next steps for your PSHE and R(S)HE journey might be. In creating this book and with the support of all of the contributors, we hope that you are as impassioned and inspired to improve the provision of PSHE and R(S)HE for all children as we are.

#PSHEisnotjustcircletime

Figures

Tables

Contributors

Victoria Pugh is a Senior Lecturer in Personal, Social, Health and Economic (PSHE) and Relationships and Sex Education (RSE) at the University of Worcester, UK, where she is undergraduate Year 2 Cohort Lead, and Special Educational Needs, Disability and Inclusion (SENDI) and Diversity Lead. She has worked as primary and middle school teacher having taught pupils from nursery to middle school. She worked as a PSHE coordinator for thirteen years as well as being a Specialist Leader of Education for PSHE in Herefordshire where she leads a PSHE network. Victoria spent a number of years working in Germany, Italy and Switzerland teaching and developing PSHE curricular for a number of schools. Her passion for PSHE has led to the development of a number of projects including a training programme for online resilience. Her passion for PSHE led her to her current role where she supports and teaches student teachers about the importance of high quality PSHE, RSE and confidence in delivering the curriculum. Victoria is the series editor and co-author of the Collins "My Life" PSHE curriculum packs.

Daniel Hughes is the PGCE Primary Course Leader at the University of Worcester, UK, lecturing in English, P.E. and outdoor education. Before working in higher education, he spent fifteen years teaching in primary schools; he has been an English subject lead for seven years and worked as a Lead Teacher for the local authority. He has set up his own private tutoring business as well as leading his own bespoke training on the teaching of writing for primary schools. Since joining the university, Daniel has worked hard to promote PSHE through English with the student teachers he supports, encouraging them to make links and see the difference integrated PSHE can make to the pupils they teach.

Richard Woolley is Professor of Education and Inclusion and Deputy Head of the School of Education at the University of Worcester, UK. Over the past thirty years, his career has included time in primary, further and higher education settings including as a SENCo and Deputy Headteacher. He has coordinated a range of subjects across the primary curriculum in medium sized and large schools. His professional and research interests include issues relating to diversity, equality and inclusion, relationships and sex education, PSHE, special educational needs and disabilities and supporting children's wellbeing.

Lorna Williams is a Senior Lecturer in Primary Education and PGCE Early Years Cohort Lead at the University of Worcester, UK, where she is Early Years Lead and Foundation Subjects Lead across Graduate and Undergraduate Initial Teacher Training. She works closely with colleagues in early years settings to promote the importance of training knowledgeable and outstanding early years practitioners. She had a highly successful teaching career in early years settings and schools for a decade. Her role as a Reception teacher and early years phase leader fuelled her passion to mentor and support student teachers and early years practitioners. This led to her pursuing an exciting career opportunity in Higher Education at the University of Worcester, UK, in Primary education in 2017.

Sharon Lannie is Module Leader for PGCE English at the University of Worcester, UK. She also supports the development of English in schools through delivering high-quality CPD in the area. Before joining the university, Sharon had a successful career as a primary teacher with a passion for teaching English; she has been Head of English in three different schools and worked as a Lead Teacher for English with the local Authority. Most recently, she co-wrote her first book 'Reading at Greater Depth in KS2' to support teachers with the trickier aspects of teaching reading. Sharon has also been PSHE lead and has used her passion for delivering PSHE through good quality texts throughout her career.

Ben Shakespeare is a Senior Lecturer in Primary Mathematics at the University of Worcester, UK, and an experienced primary teacher. Before joining the University in April 2018, he worked in Gloucestershire schools for ten years as a class teacher and has also worked as part of Senior Leadership Teams. As well as being a Mathematics subject leader for nine years, Ben is a qualified Mathematics Specialist Teacher (MaST), having been selected to take part in the government's training programme in 2012. He has enjoyed supporting student teachers, NQTs, RQTs and experienced teachers to further develop their teaching of mathematics and is passionate about doing this through the development of positive attitudes towards the subject.

Elena Lengthorn is a Senior Lecturer in Teacher Education at the University of Worcester, UK. She became a Fellow and Chartered Geographer of the Royal Geographical Society in 2014 and was awarded the Think Global 'Educator of the Year Award' in 2016. Elena has written articles on the United Nations Sustainable Development Goals for both 'Think Primary' and 'Primary Geography' magazines. Elena currently teaches primary geography, science and professional studies to ITE students and is the subject leader for PGCE Secondary Geography. She is also an active volunteer in global learning with Beacons DEC and for Teachers in Development Education.

Rebecca Saunders is an experienced primary school teacher of eighteen years. After receiving a BA Hons in English at the University of Greenwich, she then went on to complete a PGCE in primary education, with training focused primarily in teaching KS2. After teaching for eleven years as a class teacher, she then went on to develop her passion for teaching science by becoming a primary science teacher at a school, teaching Outdoor Learning and the National Curriculum for science from EYFS to Year 6. Rebecca has a keen interest in promoting the links between PSHE and science to children. She is currently the STEM and Science Subject leader at her school.

Karen Bubb is a Senior Lecturer in Primary Education at the University of Worcester, UK, and an experienced primary teacher working across Key Stage 1 and 2. Karen leads the Religious Education (RE) modules of the Initial Teacher Education courses and supports students to carry out RE-related research in local primary schools. Karen's passion for RE was sparked when teaching in a very multicultural area where religious beliefs were not talked about positively. Since joining the university Karen has developed trainee teacher's understanding of the importance of teaching RE in today's climate who will then pass on this importance to the future children they teach.

Kevin Bailey is currently the Director of 'Intouch Global Foundation' and works to support not for profit projects in the UK and internationally. He has worked as a primary teacher, university lecturer, literacy consultant and head teacher of both small rural and large urban primary schools. As a headteacher Kevin worked to establish a strong global perspective in the wider curriculum particularly through his educational partnerships in The Gambia and China. Recently he was a local advisor for the government-funded Global Learning Programme working with schools in the Midlands to embed global learning across the curriculum.

Ann Russell works as a freelance workshop facilitator, and Schools Amnesty Speaker to raise awareness of the refugee crisis and human rights issues in schools after visits to Calais and Dunkirk in 2015 and 2016 made a deep impression on her. She is also currently involved with Worcester Welcomes Refugees, supporting Syrian families settled in Worcester, whilst continuing to support work in Calais. Ann previously worked in the world of insurance and taught business studies in Ghana, before raising her family and then qualifying as a Primary teacher, taking on the Global Dimensions lead in her school.

Suzanne Allies is a Senior Lecturer at the University of Worcester, UK, where she is wellbeing coordinator. She is also Module Leader for an innovative undergraduate module, Developing Self, which encourages students to reflect on their personal, academic and professional selves, covering topics such as work–life balance and resilience. She has twenty years teaching experience in primary schools and was PSHE coordinator for over ten years in a three-form entry primary school. Suzanne's true passion is for supporting the mental health and wellbeing of university students, teachers and children. She has delivered many Staff Wellbeing workshops in a range of primary schools. She has presented on Wellbeing at the 2018 NaPTEC conference where she spoke about mindfulness in schools, drawing on her ten years' experience as a Buddhist practitioner.

Jenny Hatley is Course Leader in Education Studies at the University of Worcester, UK, focusing on social justice. Jenny taught in primary schools in both the state and independent sectors developing relationships education and global citizenship. She has been lead teacher for PSHE and Citizenship and has also worked in Sweden as Associate School Leader. Jenny has also taught in Higher Education and enjoys bringing a critical eye and research base to studies in Education.

PSHE and R(S)HE: Why Bother?

Victoria Pugh and Daniel Hughes

This book explores the ways in which quality Personal, Social, Health and Economic education (PSHE) and Relationship, (Sex) and Health Education (R(S)HE) can be used to enhance the overall curriculum. It is important to note that R(S)HE is a fundamental part of the wider PSHE curriculum and should therefore be treated as such. However, given the new statutory status of R(S)HE, we will refer to them separately within this book to ensure clarity regarding what is statutory and what is not. We would, however, urge schools, teachers and support staff to consider PSHE in its entirety in order to achieve a rich and purposeful curriculum for all. We will also refer to R(S)HE with the sex element of the title in brackets due to the fact that this is not mandatory within the new guidance with a note to say that it is highly recommended by DfE (2019: 23) who state that:

> The department continues to recommend therefore that all primary schools should have a sex education programme tailored to the age and the physical and emotional maturity of the pupils.

The aim of this book is to ensure that PSHE and R(S)HE is seen as a subject in its own right, rather than an afterthought. Although pastoral care is essential to a safe and happy learning environment, it alone, does not meet the needs of a quality PSHE and R(S)HE curriculum. Within this chapter we will explore the history of PSHE and R(S)HE, the current climate and how PSHE and R(S)HE links to other priority areas and policies. From here on, throughout the book the acronyms PSHE and R(S)HE will be used instead of the full subject title.

The history of PSHE and R(S)HE

Personal Social Education (PSE) was first identified as a cross-curricular 'dimension' in the 1990 National Curriculum. It was underpinned by five cross-curricular 'themes': economic and industrial understanding, careers education and guidance, health education, education for citizenship and environmental education. PSHE then became a non-statutory framework in 2000 following a report issued by the National Advisory Group on Personal, Social Health Education (1999) which sought to link PSHE to a number of national frameworks such as Every Child Matters (2003) and National Healthy School initiative. In 2008, the then Labour government announced that PSHE was to become statutory, but a general election was called and statutory PSHE was lost in the 'wash up'. In addition to this government funding for the National Healthy Schools was cut along with the National Teenage Pregnancy Strategy. The Department for Children, Schools and Families and the Department of Health funded a certificated national programme of PSHE Continuing Professional Development (CPD) for primary and secondary teachers and for school nurses from 2004–10 however, when funding was cut in 2010, although the course continued to run, the numbers of teachers recruited had dramatically declined.

However, the non-statutory status of PSHE led to further campaigns to ensure that all aspects of PSHE become a more regulated and included part of the primary and secondary curriculum due to an Ofsted report in 2012 entitled 'Not yet good enough; personal, social, health and economic education in schools' where it was identified that over 40 per cent of schools were graded as required improvement or inadequate in relation to the teaching of PSHE. Notably, this report only focused on schools already graded 'good' or 'outstanding', not schools judged to be below this grading. The PSHE Association championed the work of schools and continued to promote PSHE on a national level for statutory PSHE. By the end of 2016, five different cross-party Commons select committees, charities, PSHE experts, teachers, unions and parents' groups, had recommended that PSHE, including R(S)HE, should be statutory. An agreement as to what PSHE would stand for or be defined as was also required.

According to the PSHE Association (2018a) PSHE can be defined as 'the school subject that deals with real life issues affecting our children, families and communities. It's concerned with the social, health and economic realities of their lives, experiences and attitudes. It supports pupils to be healthy (mentally and physically); safe (online and offline) and equipped to thrive in their relationships and careers.' Whilst being comprehensive, this definition does not take account of the ways in which quality PSHE and R(S)HE can also contribute to raising attainment through the development of resilience, aspirations and self-belief.

The role and content of PSHE has undergone a variety of changes throughout the past twenty years in the primary curriculum, its journey littered with name changes, changing priorities and confused content. Those who have been teaching for a number of years may recognize PSHE as PHSEC, PSHEEC, PSHEE, SEAL and Sex education. These changes highlight the confused nature of priorities within the subject such as citizenship, health, sex education and emotional literacy. This lack of clarity has led to diluted objectives, lack of focus and loss of value for the subject with it often being seen as, 'airy fairy' and 'just talking about how you feel' or circle time for five minutes at the end of the day. With some elements of PSHE and R(S)HE now statutory from September 2020, it is hoped that there will be a renewed drive to clarify the purpose of PSHE and R(S)HE as well as updating and enhancing the design and delivery of this curriculum.

Citizenship has been removed to some extent from the PSHE and R(S)HE curriculum, however it is important to remember that the social strand of PSHE should incorporate not only education around friendships and so forth, but an understanding of an individual's role within wider society. It is advised that schools make time for quality citizenship education and support is available from The Association for Citizenship Teaching. This book will focus on the PSHE and R(S)HE objectives as taken from the statutory guidance as well as the PSHE Association Programme of Study where elements of citizenship are found within the 'relationships' and 'living in the wider world' strands of this programme.

Where are we now? The current context and changes in the legislation

The last guidance available for teachers on R(S)HE specifically was in 2000. Within this time, technology, societal pressures and health funding have meant that the key issues faced by children in 2020 are vastly different to those in 2000 and are continually evolving. In response to this and through consistent and constant lobbying and working for change, from organisations such as the PSHE Association, Sex Education Forum, Brook and Diversity Role Models amongst others, PSHE and R(S)HE is becoming a higher priority. This culminated in the Children and Social Work Act in 2017 which 'placed a duty on the Secretary of State for Education to make the new subjects of Relationships Education at primary and Relationships and Sex Education (R(S)HE) at secondary compulsory through regulations' (DfE, 2018). It also provided the power for the 'Secretary of State to make Personal, Social, Health and Economic Education (PSHE), or elements of the subject, mandatory in all schools' (DfE, 2018). Due to this legislation, guidance for a new statutory Relationships Education for primary and Relationships and Sex Education for secondary along with Health Education for All were published in 2019, seeking to guide schools and teachers as to what to teach. However, there is still confusion over the subject as a whole and what is included in the curriculum. In addition to this, many key elements of a quality PSHE and R(S)HE curriculum such as economic education and global sustainability are not included in this statutory requirement.

Table 1 below shows the statutory requirements of schools for Relationships Education and Relationships and Sex Education and Health Education as taken from the Relationships Education, Relationships and Sex Education (R(S)HE) and Health

Table 1 DfE (2019) Statutory Guidance

Relationships Education	Relationships and Sex Education	Health Education
All schools providing primary education, including all-through schools and middle schools (includes schools as set out in the Summary section).	All schools providing secondary education, including all-through schools and middle schools (includes schools as set out in the Summary section).	All maintained schools including schools with a sixth form, academies, free schools, non-maintained special schools and alternative provision, including pupil referral units.
		The statutory requirements to provide Health Education does not apply to independent schools – PSHE is already compulsory as independent schools must meet the Independent School Standards as set out in the Education (Independent School Standards) Regulations 2014. Independent schools, however, may find the principles in the guidance on Health Education helpful in planning an age-appropriate curriculum.

Education Statutory Guidance for governing bodies, proprietors, head teachers, principals, senior leadership teams, teachers (DfE, 2019) document. It is important to note again that while sex education is not statutory within primary education, it is advised by the PSHE Association that quality and age-appropriate sex education should be taught.

Our goals and the goals of many in the PSHE industry is to embrace the new statutory elements to the PSHE curriculum whilst continuing to campaign, develop and train teachers to feel confident in supporting the elements still required for a comprehensive and quality PSHE and R(S)HE curriculum. Although the additions of the new statutory R(S)HE curriculum are a positive step forward, they fall short of what we believe would be a comprehensive and relevant PSHE and R(S)HE curriculum, which would empower pupils to make informed choices for their lives currently and in the future. The diagram below (Fig. 1) shows just some of the relationships between PSHE, R(S)HE and wider school priorities and areas. This is by no means an exhaustive list and will be guided by school priorities and local need.

Within every school, a key priority will be that of safeguarding and inclusion for all which should underpin the PSHE and R(S)HE curriculum and general wellbeing

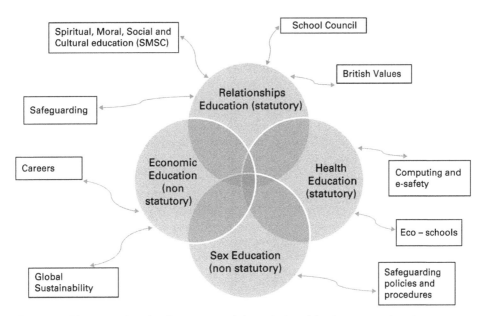

Figure 1 Diagram showing just some of the relationships between the elements of PSHE and R(S)HE and wider school priorities.

of pupils. A quality PSHE and R(S)HE curriculum can enhance the provision of safeguarding and the quality of inclusion across the school. With careful links to the Equality Act (2010), Keeping Children Safe in Education (2019), the UN Convention on the Rights of the Child (1992), British Values and SMSC, schools can embed these elements as an ethos and priority rather than a bolt-on or a one-off lesson to tick the boxes. This in turn will help to create a school culture which encourages and supports inclusion, empathy and empowerment for both children and staff.

In addition, a quality PSHE and R(S)HE curriculum can contribute to a number of areas within the current (May 2019) Education Inspection Framework (EIF). Table 2 shows some examples of EIF areas which PSHE and R(S)HE provision might support.

It is important that PSHE and R(S)HE is allotted regular and specific teaching time. Whilst this book advocates the ways in which PSHE and R(S)HE can enhance other subjects this is in addition to a clear and focused PSHE and R(S)HE curriculum as cross-curricular teaching of PSHE and R(S)HE is not enough to ensure all aspects and objectives are being covered thoroughly and that there is a progression of skills. When designing and delivering a high-quality PSHE and R(S)HE curriculum, it is essential that the relevant objectives are the primary focus of the lesson, and not shoehorned into another subject diluting the quality of the session and learning opportunities. These subjects can be used as vehicles to support delivering PSHE and R(S)HE in authentic and real-life situations, enabling pupils to think about the wider world and their place within it rather than a quick fix to fit in PSHE and R(S)HE objectives.

Table 2 Statement of judgement taken from EIF (2019)

Behaviour and Attitudes

Learners' attitudes to their education or training are positive. They are committed to their learning, know how to study effectively and do so, are resilient to setbacks and take pride in their achievements.

Relationships among learners and staff reflect a positive and respectful culture. Leaders, teachers and learners create an environment where bullying, peer-on-peer abuse or discrimination are not tolerated. If they do occur, staff deal with issues quickly and effectively, and do not allow them to spread.

Personal Development

The curriculum extends beyond the academic, technical or vocational. It provides for learners' broader development, enabling them to develop and discover their interests and talents.

The curriculum and the provider's wider work support learners to develop their character – including their resilience, confidence and independence – and help them know how to keep physically and mentally healthy.

At each stage of education, the provider prepares learners for future success in their next steps

The provider prepares learners for life in modern Britain by: – equipping them to be responsible, respectful, active citizens who contribute positively to society – developing their understanding of fundamental British values – developing their understanding and appreciation of diversity – celebrating what we have in common and promoting respect for the different protected characteristics as defined in law.

Leadership and Management

Leaders have a clear and ambitious vision for providing high-quality, inclusive education and training to all. This is realised through strong, shared values, policies and practice.

Leaders engage effectively with learners and others in their community, including – where relevant – parents, carers, employers and local services.

Those with responsibility for governance ensure that the provider fulfils its statutory duties, for example under the Equality Act 2010, and other duties, for example in relation to the 'Prevent' strategy and safeguarding, and promoting the welfare of learners.

The provider has a culture of safeguarding that supports effective arrangements to:
– identify learners who may need early help or who are at risk of neglect, abuse, grooming or exploitation
– help learners reduce their risk of harm by securing the support they need, or referring in a timely way to those who have the expertise to help.

Consulting with parents and carers

Within the Relationships Education, Relationships and Sex Education (RSE) and Health Education DfE guidance document (DfE, 2019: 11), the importance of consulting with parents/carers is clearly outlined, stating that, 'Schools must consult parents in developing and reviewing their policy'. Additionally, it comments that, 'All schools should work closely with parents when planning and delivering these subjects. Schools should ensure that parents know what will be taught and when, and clearly communicate the fact that parents have the right to request that their child be withdrawn from some or all of sex education delivered as part of statutory RSE' (DfE, 2019: 17). Research undertaken by Wright and Wooden (2012) highlighted that parent involvement in sex education positively impacted upon communication and parent–child relationships. In particular, Turnbull et al. (2008) report that whilst research shows that children and young people want to discuss issues surrounding sex and relationships with parents, and parent want to hold these conversations, it was the parents who found the idea embarrassing and felt they lacked the skills to be able to deal with these conversations effectively. Therefore, seemingly, there is an opportunity with the changes to statutory R(S)HE and DfE guidance for schools to help bridge this gap. PSHE coordinators and school leadership may have concerns surrounding how best to collect feedback from parents/carers, relay information regarding statutory requirements and ensuring positive communication throughout the process, however this opportunity is one which can lead to strong partnerships. Guidance for parental involvement has been issued by the DfE in their publication 'Parental Engagement on Relationships Education' (DfE, 2019), this guidance outlines what parents should be consulted on, tips for how and case studies as examples, and a link can be found in the Key reading section at the end of the chapter.

Strategies and examples of parental engagement

Some strategies which might help to support parental engagement include:

- Developing a strong partnership with parents throughout the year using drop-in evenings, celebration assembly, information evenings, parent/carer story sessions, parents/carers as careers speakers, Parent, Teacher, Friends Associations, etc.
- Clear guidance on what is deemed as relationships education (i.e. objectives within the DfE guidance) and what sessions constitute sex education, which will be taught in addition to the relationship objectives. It is important to note that puberty is now a statutory part of Health education. Having clear communication around what is statutory and what parents can withdraw their children from, can help parents to make informed decisions on what they feel is best for their child.
- Sending out a recommended book list to parents/carers a couple of months prior to specific sex education lessons gives them time to reflect upon the fact that their child/children are growing up and be involved in how best to support them by buying a book which they can look at with their child or give to the child to read independently. It is a great idea to have copies of the recommended books which

should cover both puberty and sex education. These can be kept in a box in the school office or a shared place where pupils can view them without having to make an appointment. This way they can choose the books they feel are most appropriate for their child or alternatively choose to initiate conversations themselves.

- Prior to specific sex education lessons, you may wish to invite parents in to view the PSHE and R(S)HE curriculum resources as a whole rather than just R(S) HE which might make parents/carers feel uncomfortable. This type of session can include activities which parents/carers can take part in from the curriculum plans, a review of resources and time for questions if needed. These questions can be carried out in the same way in which we would with pupils through the use of an 'ask it basket' this way parents/carers can anonymously ask the questions they want to and the teacher can assess them prior to answering. This is particularly helpful as it avoids teachers being 'put on the spot' or answering questions which they don't feel are appropriate.

- If an external visitor is brought in to teach sex education i.e. a school nurse, it is vital that they are involved in speaking to and supporting parents/carers. It is also key that teachers receive training on sex education and how to answer questions relating to content as pupils need to be able to ask questions which pupils have at other times when the school nurse is not present.

- If an interactive session isn't possible due to time, parental engagement levels or staffing, resources can be put into a box which again can be placed in a shared place or for a period of time for parents/carers to view. This transparency of what is being taught and the resources used can be incredibly reassuring for parents, some of which will have a limited knowledge of the R(S)HE curriculum or have a knowledge based upon media depictions – which we all know can be misleading at best. In essence, parents/carers just want to know that their children aren't accessing inappropriate content such as pornography or resources which might be harmful and accessing learning materials upfront is an effective way to ease any possible concerns they might have.

- If parents/carers still do not feel comfortable with their child attending sex education lessons they can be invited to speak to the PSHE coordinator who will be able to go into more detail about the curriculum content. It can also be useful to remind parents/carers that pupils will hear sex education-related 'facts' and discussions on the playground, at clubs and outside of school and these can cause many misconceptions which could be detrimental to the pupils understanding of healthy relationships. Therefore, the best place for them to receive this education is at home or in school where the sessions focus on healthy relationships, consent, choice and facts.

In conclusion, only Relationships and Health education will be mandatory from September 2020, however, we are in agreeance with the PSHE Association (2018b:

12) that states: 'To be effective, RSE should always be taught within a broader PSHE education programme.' Although we have separated the terms PSHE and R(S)HE for the purposes of clarity throughout the book, these should be considered as one with PSHE consisting of R(S)HE and other wider issues such as careers, environmental sustainability, economics education and citizenship in order to meet the needs of pupils and school community. All too often, PSHE and R(S)HE is focused on one aspect in particular – circle time! Despite being a useful tool for discussion around key topics and issues, it is not PSHE education. Through the case studies and examples within the book, we will explore how PSHE and R(S)HE is so much more than just circle time; it is a subject that deserves to be valued as a subject that can prepare children for life and its challenges.

Key reading

- DfE (2019), *Relationships Education, Relationships and Sex Education (RSE) and Health Education.* Available online: https://assets.publishing.service.gov.uk/government/uploads/system/uploads/attachment_data/file/805781/Relationships_Education__Relationships_and_Sex_Education__RSE__and_Health_Education.pdf (accessed 20 September 2019).

Further reading

- Ofsted (2019), *The education inspection framework.* Available online: https://assets.publishing.service.gov.uk/government/uploads/system/uploads/attachment_data/file/801429/Education_inspection_framework.pdf (accessed 20 September 2019).

References

DCSF (2003), *Every Child Matters.* Available online: https://assets.publishing.service.gov.uk/government/uploads/system/uploads/attachment_data/file/272064/5860.pdf (accessed 5 September 2019) (accessed 20 September 2019).

DfE (2018), *Relationships Education, Relationships and Sex Education, and Health Education.* Available online: https://consult.education.gov.uk/pshe/relationships-education-rse-health-education/ (accessed 20 September 2019).

(DfE (2019) *Parental engagement on relationships education.* Available online: https://assets.publishing.service.gov.uk/government/uploads/system/uploads/attachment_ data/file/884450/Parental_engagement_on_relationships_education.pdf (accessed 19 September 2019).

DfE (2019), *Relationships Education, Relationships and Sex Education (RSE) and Health Education*. Available online: https://assets.publishing.service.gov.uk/government/uploads/system/uploads/attachment_data/file/805781/Relationships_Education__Relationships_and_Sex_Education__RSE__and_Health_Education.pdf (accessed 19 September 2019).

H.M. Treasury (2003), *Every child matters: presented to Parliament by the Chief Secretary to the Treasury by command of Her Majesty*, Norwich: The Stationary Office.

National Advisory Group on Personal, Social and Health Education (Nottingham, England) (1999), *Preparing young people for adult life: a report by the National Advisory Group on Personal, Social and Health Education*, Nottingham: DFEE.

Ofsted (2012), *Not yet good enough: personal, social, health and economic education in schools*. Available online: https://assets.publishing.service.gov.uk/government/uploads/system/uploads/attachment_data/file/413178/Not_yet_good_enough_personal__social__health_and_economic_education_in_schools.pdf (accessed 18 September 2019).

Ofsted (2019) *The education inspection framework*. Available online: https://assets.publishing.service.gov.uk/government/uploads/system/uploads/attachment_data/file/801429/Education_inspection_framework.pdf (accessed 17 March 2020).

PSHE Association (2018a), *PSHE education: a guide for parents*. Available online: https://www.pshe-association.org.uk/pshe-education-guide-parents (accessed 19 September 2019).

PSHE Association (2018b), *Preparing for statutory RSE and relationships education within your PSHE curriculum*. Available online: https://www.pshe-association.org.uk/curriculum-and-resources/resources/preparing-statutory-rse-and-relationships (accessed 12 March 2020)

Turnbull, T., van Wersch, A. and van Schaik, P. (2008), 'A review of parental involvement in sex education: The role for effective communication in British families', *Health Education Journal*, 67: 182–95.

UK Public General Acts (2017), *Children and Social Work Act*. Available online: http://www.legislation.gov.uk/ukpga/2017/16/introduction/enacted (accessed 19 September 2019).

Wright, K. N. and Wooden, C. (2012), 'A qualitative assessment of a parent-developed, parent-run program to prevent teenage pregnancy', *Journal of Human Behavior in the Social Environment*, 22 (1): 85–100.

1

We're All in this Together!

Victoria Pugh

This chapter explores:

- A whole school approach to PSHE and R(S)HE;
- It will highlight the importance of strong leadership and coordination in this area and where to begin if a teacher is new to the role, including key elements to policy writing;
- It will explore the ways in which PSHE and R(S)HE can be assessed effectively to support pupils and highlight progress.

Leadership and coordination

The coordination and leadership of PSHE can be a dauting task, particularly in light of the new guidance for Relationship, (Sex) and Health education, (R(S)HE), however it should be viewed as an opportunity rather than a struggle. The recent changes in legislation allow for a focus on the evaluation, revision and implementation of an updated, engaging curriculum, which can be adapted to meet the needs of both the pupils and the local community.

The Department for Education (DfE) guidance on R(S)HE (2019: 16) states that governors and school management must ensure strong leadership and that the subject is, 'resourced, staffed and timetabled in a way that ensures that the school can fulfil its legal obligation'. In accordance with this, it is vital that schools prepare for R(S)HE and other areas of PSHE such as economic education utilizing a whole-school approach. This approach must consider training for governors, headteachers, teachers and support staff as well as a comprehensive policy which encompasses the voice of all stakeholders. This is made clear in the government guidance which states

'All schools must have in place a written policy for Relationships Education and RSE. Schools must consult parents in developing and reviewing their policy.' (2019:11)

There have been a number of studies exploring a whole-school approach to PSHE including work by Public Health England which discusses the benefits as:

> taking a whole-school approach to health and well-being is linked to pupils' readiness to learn. A review of the links between pupil health and well-being and attainment advocated promotion of health and well-being as an essential element of a school's effectiveness strategy.
>
> Public Health England, 2014: 10

The need for a well-structured and robust whole-school approach can also be seen from Ofsted guidance regarding the statutory elements of Relationship and health education with Roary Pownall, Ofsted's National Lead for PSHE and for Citizenship reminding schools of paragraph 220 and 221 of the school inspection handbook (2019: 220) which states:

> From September 2019, schools are able to follow a new relationships and sex education and health education curriculum. Primary-age children must be taught about positive relationships and respect for others, and how these are linked to promoting good mental health and well-being ... And If a school is failing to meet its obligations, inspectors will consider this when reaching the personal development judgement.

It, therefore, goes without saying that providing a quality PSHE and R(S)HE curriculum within schools can strongly enhance safeguarding by both empowering pupils to be able to keep themselves safe as well as knowing where to go for help or assistance if needed. As already discussed in the introductory chapter of this book, a quality whole-school approach to PSHE and R(S)HE which takes into consideration school priorities such as safeguarding, SMSC, British Values and quality can support schools in ensuring an 'outstanding' personal development, behaviour and attitudes and leadership and management judgements by Ofsted.

Case Study 1

Ahmed is a Year 1 teacher and works in a large three-form entry primary school which is a values-led school. He is new to the role of PSHE coordinator and is feeling very overwhelmed by the new statutory guidance as well as the fact that R(S)HE and Health education are part of the school improvement plan. He has some experience of teaching PSHE, however there has never been a planned, assessed and monitored programme of study and the school are keen to have some consistency across the school to ensure they are meeting the statutory objectives. He has carried out an initial audit of the schools PSHE lessons and found that a number of classes are focusing mainly on circle time to deliver PSHE and other classes are not carrying out any PSHE at all with some teachers stating that there just isn't time for PSHE particularly in upper KS2 where they are concentrating on SATS preparation. Ahmed cannot monitor pupil's progression in PSHE and R(S)HE skills as the teaching seems to be done in an 'ad hoc' fashion. Ahmed hasn't received any PSHE or R(S)HE training and is finding it difficult to work out where to start in relation to a whole-school approach.

Where to start?

It can be easy for teachers, regardless of experience, to feel overwhelmed when taking over the coordination of a subject across a key stage or school particularly if the coordinator themselves doesn't feel confident with the subject area. It can often be the case that recently qualified teachers are given the role of PSHE coordinator or those who are deemed as more 'pastoral' in nature; however given the complexity of the topics which PSHE and R(S)HE covers this can often leave coordination of the subject in the hands of teachers who do not have the training or experience to feel they can confidently manage the subject. Nevertheless, coordination should not be seen as an unmanageable task, instead a good place for Ahmed to start would be to find out what PSHE and R(S)HE is being delivered at present and how. This information can be collected through the use of simple teacher/ support staff questionnaires which ask questions such as:

- What PSHE and R(S)HE topics or issues are you currently teaching within your year group or class?
- In what ways is PSHE and R(S)HE taught within your year group or class? E.g. whole-class discussion, separate PSHE lesson, through cross-curricular units.
- How confident do you feel teaching PSHE?
- What training would you like to receive in order to feel more confident when planning, delivering and assessing PSHE and R(S)HE?
- What resources do you feel would be beneficial to support the teaching of PSHE and R(S)HE?

Feedback from staff can allow the coordinator to gain a picture of the current climate of PSHE and R(S)HE within the school quickly, assess where the gaps are and begin to put in place an action plan for curriculum development, training and resourcing. This information can also be used to inform the development of a school PSHE and R(S)HE policy (these can be separate or combined) which includes the voice of governors, senior leadership team, teachers, support staff, parents, current and past pupils. Forming a working party to discuss key areas (see Table 3) can lead to the formation of a cohesive, inclusive and accessible policy ensuring that the voices of all stakeholders are united. It can be powerful to invite both current and past pupils to contribute to these discussions as often past pupils will be able to give honest feedback about the quality of PSHE and R(S)HE education they received and whether or not they felt this was adequate enough to support them with the transition to their next phase of schooling such as junior school or high school.

Once Ahmed has a clear picture of the current provision for PSHE and R(S) HE within the school he can begin to look at policy writing. According to the PSHE Association (2018: 12), a PSHE policy serves a number of purposes:

- It offers a whole-school statement of intent through its aims for PSHE.
- It sets out an agreed approach to PSHE in the curriculum, guiding practice, offering a clear framework for teaching and a 'toolkit' for future decision-making.
- It clarifies the school's intended outcomes for its PSHE provision.
- It informs and reflects practice by outlining the content covered and methodology used to enable learning in PSHE.

This is the same when considering writing a PSHE and R(S)HE policy. It is important to have a shared understanding of what the policy will cover and that key decisions regarding specific R(S)HE issues are clearly communicated so that they can be followed and understood by all stakeholders. The Relationships Education, Relationships and Sex Education (RSE) and Health Education (2019: 11) guidance states that:

All schools must have an up-to-date policy, which is made available to parents and others. Schools must provide a copy of the policy free of charge to anyone who asks for one and should publish the policy on the school website.

This specifically refers to the R(S)HE elements as a statutory obligation, however, having a policy which incorporates both R(S)HE and PSHE shows clear links to the ways in which R(S)HE is taught within a broader PSHE curriculum.

The DfE statutory guidance (2019:17) further states:

Parents should be given every opportunity to understand the purpose and content of Relationships Education and RSE. Good communication and opportunities for parents to understand and ask questions about the school's approach help increase confidence in the curriculum.

In order to foster this partnership, it is important that parents/carers are included in the formation of the PSHE and R(S)HE policy as well as being privy to the planning materials and resources which the school will be using. This transparency can help parents/carers to be fully informed of what and how relationships and sex education will be taught throughout the school, how it contributes to the broader PSHE curriculum, therefore dispelling any myths which might circulate about the content of the lessons.

Although parents/carers have the right to withdraw their children from the Sex Education element due to the fact that it has not been included in the statutory guidance, a number of organizations such as the Sex Education Forum and PSHE Association show support for the teaching of Sex Education with the Family Planning Association (2019) stating that 'We believe all children and young people have a fundamental right to high quality, comprehensive relationship and sex education, which promotes good sexual health and equal and enjoyable relationships.'

Some specific R(S)HE considerations might include discussions around the following which should be included within a school's policy:

- A definition of Relationships Education and Sex Education (if you choose to include this in your curriculum which it is strongly advised that you do). This is important to clarify which parts of the curriculum fall under Relationships education and which part fall under Sex education from which pupils can be withdrawn.
- When scientific vocabulary for body parts will be introduced?
- Which scheme of work or content will be followed for PSHE and R(S)HE?
- The structure of PSHE and R(S)HE education and how it will be taught.
- The procedures which will be followed if parents wish to withdraw their child from Sex Education lessons (remembering that Relationships Education is statutory, and pupils cannot be withdrawn from these lessons).
- What resources will be used?
- How will visiting speakers or organizations be chosen and how will the school ensure that they deliver appropriate material.

In addition, the policy and provision provided must be sensitive to local need. For example, if there are particularly high rates of domestic violence within the school community this should be reflected in the curriculum provided perhaps by ensuring a spiral strand of lessons which deal with what a healthy/unhealthy relationship looks like, where to go for help if a child doesn't feel safe at home and sessions covering self-esteem. Statistics and data can be found from NHS data, census surveys and demographic data from data.gov.uk, which can help to ascertain the local needs of your setting.

When developing a PSHE and R(S)HE policy the prompts given in Table 3 may prove to be useful.

A more detailed 'how to' guide for policy writing is available from the PSHE Association with both individual and school membership for a low yearly fee. This gives you access to a range of resources and policy toolkits which can be used to create a PSHE and R(S)HE policy. A number of PSHE schemes of work will come with policy templates provided and these can be adapted to suit the needs of the pupils and the school.

Table 3 Developing a PSHE and R(S)HE policy

What to include	Consider
Rationale	What is the purpose of the policy? Who has written it and who has been consulted or involved in its development? When was it written? When will it be reviewed? Who will review it? What definition of Relationships Education or PSHE are you using throughout your policy?
Links to other policies	How does this policy link to other school and national policies and guidance. E.g. Keeping Children Safe in Education (2019), Prevent Duty (2019) School safeguarding policy (the policy should clearly state what staff should do in the event of a disclosure) Equality Act (2010), SMSC, British Values, Drug and Alcohol policy, RE policy, Computing Policy.
Curriculum Content	What will be taught? When will it be taught? – a table of yearly units or content is useful here. Who will teach PSHE and R(S)HE? How will it be taught? What strategies, techniques or pedagogy will be utilized to ensure quality delivery of PSHE and opportunities for learning. What resources will be used? How will PSHE and R(S)HE be assessed? How will you ensure that your curriculum and teaching are fully inclusive so that PSHE content can be accessed by all pupils? If you are using a scheme or programme of study it is likely that there will be a mapping document which clearly shows objectives or skills which will be met and progression of these throughout the year groups. This is a great way to clearly show progression through the school and identify the expectations of subject coverage, knowledge and skills in each year group.
Parents/carers/ guardian right to withdraw	What are parents/carers/guardians' rights to withdraw their child from lessons? Which lessons can they withdraw them from? How to they do this? What will the child do instead? How will parent/carers/guardians be involved in discussions around PSHE and R(S)HE. How will their input be used?

> ## Reflection
>
> - Will the scientific names for private body parts such as vagina, vulva and penis be introduced from Reception year or later in KS1? This vocabulary should be agreed upon by all stakeholders and used consistently.
> - How will PSHE and R(S)HE be planned into your timetable to ensure that it builds upon content and skills each year in a spiral format rather than a series of one-off lessons or drop-down days.
> - What are the next steps for your setting in relation developing a quality PSHE and R(S)HE policy and what support do you need from leadership/colleagues in order to facilitate this?
> - How will you ensure that the voices of all relevant stakeholders are evident within your policy and how will this be managed?

Creating a spiral curriculum and assessment

According to the PSHE Association (2014) ten principles of PSHE education, it is important to 'plan a "spiral programme" which introduces new and more challenging learning, whilst building on what has gone before to reflect and meets the personal developmental needs of the children and young people.' This allows for the development of skills as well as knowledge of specific content rather than popular 'drop-down days' where pupils have a focused day on a particular topic and then have no opportunity to revisit the topic in the future.

Johnston (2012: 224) deems the benefits of a spiral curriculum as 'allow[ing] a logical progression from simplistic ideas to complicated ideas'.

An example of this can be seen in the following Relationships Education objective:

- The importance of respecting others, even when they are very different from them (for example, physically, in character, personality or backgrounds), or make different choices or have different preferences or beliefs.

This objective can be introduced in Year 1 allowing pupils to think about the things they like and dislike and how these differ from their peers and friends: this can then be developed in Year 3 by thinking about what respect means and how it can be shown on a day-to-day basis by drawing/discussing situations where pupils disagree

Case Study 2

Nadia is a Year 6 teacher who is an experienced PSHE coordinator. She feels confident that the schools PSHE and R(S)HE policy is clear and covers all the requires sections as advised by the PSHE Association and DfE *Relationships Education, Relationships and Sex Education (RSE) and Health Education Statutory Guidance* (2019) document. The school are following a PSHE and R(S)HE scheme of work and are happy that the coverage meets the needs of the pupils, is spiral and inclusive in its design. The one area which Nadia is struggling with is assessment. Current PSHE and R(S)HE are not being assessed and this means that it is difficult to get an overall picture of pupils' progress and confidence in the subject. Nadia's headteacher has given her the task of exploring assessment strategies which the whole school can adopt to ensure consistency throughout the school.

Nadia's situation is not an uncommon one. Although not always seen as a 'traditional' subject which requires assessment, it is important to note that in order to provide quality PSHE and R(S)HE there must be opportunities for assessment in order to ensure that pupils progress in both knowledge and skills.

The PSHE Association's 'A guide to assessment in primary education' (2020) document outlines a three-step assessment model focusing on baseline assessment, assessment for learning and assessment of learning. Given that the DfE states in the statutory guidance for Relationships, Sex and Health education (2019) states that 'schools should have the same high expectations of the quality of pupils' work in these subjects as for other curriculum areas' seemingly, this will become even more crucial with the introduction of statutory R(S)HE.

A key element of the examples shown in Figure 2 are that they provide inclusive assessment opportunities which allow the pupils to showcase their knowledge and skills to the highest degree. By utilizing a range of assessment methods a Universal Design for Learning (UDL) model can be achieved to ensure inclusion for all (see www.CAST.org for more information). All of these examples offer opportunities for pupils to revisit their work and amend it to show what they have learnt. For example, at the beginning of a unit of work around 'healthy friendships' pupils could be asked to share their thoughts on what they know already about what a healthy friendship looks like. They could draw and write about it or show it as a cartoon strip. At the end of the lesson or unit of study these could then be revisited and annotated to show what they now know about healthy friendships and reflect upon how their ideas might have changed or evolved. This would allow Nadia and her colleagues to record progression based upon a baseline example and revisited work. Where work is based upon character education or personal

Figure 2 Examples of assessment activities.

attributes self-assessment strategies can be employed to give pupils occasion to self-reflect through a journal entry style assessment or by sharing their thoughts on sticky notes which can form a class discussion display.

with each other and how these situations can be resolved. In upper KS2 this can be further developed to think about equality and researching famous activists and people who changed the world by challenging equality such as Rosa Parks, Malala Yousafzai or Mahatma Gandhi. This can be an interesting way in which to allow discussions around what happens when people aren't respectful of people's choices or beliefs. But, how can pupils' understanding, and reflections of this knowledge, be assessed to show this progression in learning?

Reflection

- How will your setting ensure that teaching and learning is spiral in nature, building upon skills and knowledge?
- What methods of assessment are currently being used and are these consistent throughout the setting?
- Is the assessment being used more evaluative in nature or is it truly assessing progress?
- How does your assessment promote inclusion for all? Can your assessment methods be more creative or diverse to meet the needs of pupils or allow them to represent their learning in a way which is meaningful for them?

Points to consider and conclusion

Taking a whole-school approach to PSHE and R(S)HE is essential for quality planning, delivery and assessment. Discussions with a range of staff, parents/carers, governors and pupils – past and present, are the key to developing a PSHE and R(S) HE programme, which will really meet the needs of the pupils and local community. A whole-school audit can be an effective way to begin, as it will help to identify the great practice already in place and the areas for development. The introduction of statutory Relationships and Sex Education and Health Education does not mean that schools need to start from scratch, merely that some form of mapping to identify the objectives already being met and those which need to be included is carried out. Staff and governor training are crucial to create a whole-school ethos and confidence surrounding the rationale behind PSHE and R(S)HE education and the decisions being made regarding bespoke content for the school. Inclusive assessment opportunities will provide teachers with a more in-depth awareness of pupil understanding and progress allowing for a PSHE and R(S)HE curriculum which feeds forward to facilitate pupil progress. This type of assessment will 'allow the leadership team, parents, governors and school inspectors to see the impact PSHE education is having for pupils and for whole-school outcomes, such as Ofsted and ISI judgements on personal development, safeguarding, SMSC development and the promotion of fundamental British values. Without assessing PSHE education all you can do is describe provision; you cannot show its impact.' (PSHE Association, 2020: 2). It is imperative that PSHE and R(S)HE coordinators utilize feedback or ideas to enhance the curriculum or practice within the school and embrace the new changes for what they are – an exciting opportunity for us to provide excellent life education skills for our pupils.

Points to consider for your setting

- How confident do you as teachers feel about both the content of the new statutory guidance and other aspects of PSHE such as economic education and global education?
- How have you ensured that the PSHE and R(S)HE curriculum you are following or have designed meets the needs of your pupils and the wider community? What data have you used to ascertain what these needs might be?
- How will you encourage parents/carers and the wider community to be actively involved in the formation of PSHE and R(S)HE policies, content and revision?
- How will your setting assess PSHE and R(S)HE and ensure not only that it is inclusive, but that it shows the impact of the PSHE and R(S)HE curriculum?

Key reading

- CAST (2020), *About Universal Design for Learning.* Available online: http://www.cast.org/our-work/about-udl.html (accessed 21 September 2019).
- PSHE Association (2020), *Primary assessment guide.* Available online: https://www.pshe-association.org.uk/curriculum-and-resources/resources/guides-assessment-pshe-education-ks1-4 (accessed 5 March 2020).

Further reading

- Cowley, S. (2018), *The ultimate guide to differentiation: achieving excellence for all,* London: Bloomsbury.
- Florian, L. and Beaton, M. (2018), 'Inclusive pedagogy in action: getting it right for every child', *International Journal of Inclusive Education,* 22 (8): 870–84.

References

Department for Education (2019), *Relationships Education, Relationships and Sex Education (RSE) and Health Education: statutory guidance for governing bodies, proprietors, head teachers, principals, senior leadership teams, teachers*, London: Department for Education.

Family Planning Association (2019), 'Relationships and Sex Education: What's Changing'. Available online: https://www.fpa.org.uk/news/relationships-and-sex-education-what%E2%80%99s-changing (accessed 21 September 2019).

Johnston, H. (2012), *The spiral curriculum: Research into practice*. Available online: https://files.eric.ed.gov/fulltext/ED538282.pdf (accessed 27 September 2019).

Ofsted (2019) *The education inspection framework*. Available online: https://assets.publishing.service.gov.uk/government/uploads/system/uploads/attachment_data/file/801429/Education_inspection_framework.pdf (accessed 17 March 2020).

PSHE Association (2014), *Planning for a spiral curriculum*. Available online: https://www.pshe-association.org.uk/curriculum-and-resources/curriculum (accessed 1 September 2019).

PSHE Association (2018), *Preparing for statutory RSE and relationships education within your PSHE curriculum*. Available online: https://www.pshe-association.org.uk/curriculum-and-resources/resources/preparing-statutory-rse-and-relationships

PSHE Association (2020), *Primary assessment guide*. Available online: https://www.pshe-association.org.uk/curriculum-and-resources/resources/guides-assessment-pshe-education-ks1-4 (accessed on 5 March 2020)

Public Health England (2014), *The link between pupil health and wellbeing and attainment; A briefing for head teachers, governors and staff in education settings*. Available online: https://assets.publishing.service.gov.uk/government/uploads/system/uploads/attachment_data/file/370686/HT_briefing_layoutvFINALvii.pdf (accessed 1 September 2019).

2

Controversial Issues in PSHE and R(S)HE

Richard Woolley

This chapter explores:

- Strategies for tackling controversial issues in the classroom;
- Why an issue may be controversial;
- The use of labels and labelling and how this can be done appropriately.

Each of us has issues that we find difficult to discuss. These may be because of past experiences, being unsure about our own viewpoints, being worried about causing offence or saying the wrong thing, or the fact that the issue is new to us. The same is true within our professional context and it is important to consider what can make an issue controversial within the setting of the primary school, particularly in the areas of Personal, Social, Health and Economic Education and Relationships Education. There are several reasons for issues feeling controversial (Woolley, 2010; 2020), including because:

- they challenge the status quo, for example relating to gender, identity, racism, family structures. This can include discussing issues about which children's parents and carers may have strongly held views;
- they make us feel uncomfortable, possibly though unfamiliarity with the content, not having discussed them before or our own personal experience. For example, how our bodies change as we grow up, bereavement or family separation and divorce;
- there are questions about age-appropriateness, for example at what age or stage of development is it appropriate to talk with children about how their bodies

will change during puberty, how a baby is conceived, or different romantic and sexual relationships that people may experience; and

- they may be felt to be political, for example issues that children encounter in the news including war, famine, poverty and civil disobedience.

One area that teachers regularly identify as being of concern is the use of labels and specific terms when referring to people and their identities. This chapter explores this area through case studies, one which focuses on the terms used to identify body parts, and another that explores the terms used for gender identity.

Strategies for tackling controversial issues

Having a toolkit of strategies for tackling sensitive, tricky or controversial issues provides scaffolding to help navigate through issues as they arise. It is important to remember that sometimes it is wise to indicate that a child's question is important, but cannot be discussed straight away. Indicating 'That is a really good question. Can we talk about it later?' provides a window of opportunity to think carefully about what needs to be discussed, to consult with a colleague, the head teacher or the child's parent/carer, and to reflect on how any subject matter relates to school policies. Of course, it is important to return to the child's question at a later point so that they know it was valued. This is one example of a distancing technique, which provides the teacher with space to reflect and consider their response to a child. Setting ground rules, where all involved in a discussion understand that they need not answer personal questions or disclose personal information is also important in enabling all involved to feel safe and respected.

Strategies may be rooted in whole-school policies, in-service training, schemes of work or programmes of study and individual lessons. Specific approaches can include (extended from Woolley, 2010: 10–11):

- Engaging in a campaign
- Involving visits and visitors
- Forging international links
- Visualization
- Role play
- Communities of enquiry
- Debates and *Philosophy for Children* (see https://p4c.com/)
- Buddying
- Children's picture books and stories
- Circle time.

Whilst there is not the opportunity to explore each of these in detail within this chapter, signposting such strategies provides the opportunity for you to engage in further reading and investigation. The case studies that follow provide two examples to illustrate such approaches.

Case Study 1: Key Stage 1

Children in Year 2 have been engaging in a series of lessons identifying body parts and their correct names.

Martha has considered carefully how she will introduce the anatomically correct names for body parts across a series of lessons with her Year 2 class. The children are used to engaging in activities sitting in a circle, and Martha feels that the familiarity and security of the circle is a positive and supportive environment in which to introduce vocabulary. In the first lesson she starts with some introductory level sharing activities, passing a bean bag and asking the children to name their favourite colour and the favourite activity in which they engage out of school. This warm-up ensures that the children are settled and calm, so that hopefully any awkwardness or embarrassment in the next section of the lesson will be minimized. The circle ensures that all children can see and hear each other, as well as giving Martha an ideal opportunity to see that they are all settled and engaged.

Using *Amazing You!* (Saltz, 2008) Martha starts by asking the children to name the parts of the human body that we can see. This leads into an explanation about the parts of our bodies that we call the private parts, 'because they stay hidden under your clothes or underwear. They belong to you and they are special' (Saltz, 2008: 5). She uses the book to support talk within the circle about the different names we use for our private parts, acknowledging the normality of this and also explaining that there are medically correct terms that the children are now old enough and mature enough to know and to use. The book explains how our bodies change over time. It begins to introduce human reproduction, but without specific detail about sexual intercourse. The book indicates that it is intended for pre-schoolers, and so the language and content are certainly appropriate for this Year 2 class.

This lesson builds on the statutory requirement within the *National Curriculum in England* that children in Year 1 should 'identify, name, draw and label the basic parts of the human body and say which part of the body is associated with each sense' (DfE, 2013: 149). It also relates to the requirement of the statutory guidance for *Relationships and Sex Education* (DfE, 2019) that by the end of primary school pupils should know 'that each person's body belongs to them, and the differences between appropriate and inappropriate or unsafe physical, and other, contact' (2019: 22).

The naming of body parts using words we might use then speaking with a doctor or nurse normalizes such vocabulary, so that it is not a surprise nor an embarrassment when such terms are introduced during lessons later in Key Stage 2 and indeed beyond. Generally, the words are no more complicated to say than the informal or slang words used outside of the classroom. It may be that adults involved in such lessons are not particularly used to using anatomically correct words themselves and will wish to make sure that they feel confident, and do not feel embarrassed, themselves. Sometimes the things we want to avoid discussing with the children in our classrooms have more to do with our own feelings and insecurities than those of the children.

The use of appropriate terms enables children to communicate clearly, as the following example illustrates. Sheila is a teaching assistant working with a Key Stage 1 class. During a training session on PSHE she explains to a group of colleagues a situation that arose in her school. One child, Sara, had mentioned on several occasions that her grandad asked to see her flower. The staff thought nothing of this, as during the course of the topic for the term the children had been tending the garden, learning about nature and decorating Mother's Day cards, often talking about flowers. They took home flowers made in class as gifts for close relatives and friends. It was only when she realized that Sara use the word 'flower' to refer to her genitals that Sheila realized that she needed to raise a safeguarding issue. Had Sara had the correct terminology to use, this issue would have been identified far sooner.

A resource that Martha could use in later lessons with her Year 2 class is the NSPCC's 'Let's Talk PANTS' campaign (launched in 2016) which helps to support adults when talking to children about how to stay safe. It identifies some key messages and provides resources to discuss these with young children:

P = Privates are private
A = Always remember your body belongs to you
N = No means no
T = Talk about secrets that upset you
S = Speak up, someone can help you (NSPCC, 2019)

The NSPCC provides guides for parents/carers and others to support conversations with their child, which will also be helpful to teachers and others in the children's workforce. They emphasize the need to avoid scaring children. Its website notes that:

It's a difficult thing to think about but we know that children are sometimes sexually abused by adults who are family members and by people who are known to them. They can also be sexually abused by young people. You don't want to alarm or distress your child and anything you say should be age appropriate for your child. When talking PANTS with your children you should always emphasise that if <u>anyone</u> (even a member of the family or friend) touches them in an inappropriate way or makes them feel uncomfortable, they should tell an adult they trust.

NSPCC, 2019

Reflection

Reflecting on the issues raised in the Key Stage 1 case study, consider:

- how using formal terminology for body parts can support both clear communication and an appropriate tone of discussion in the classroom;
- how to enable children to understand that in conversation outside the classroom people sometimes choose to use informal language when speaking about their bodies;
- the importance of helping children to understand that our behaviours can be context-specific e.g. we may get fully undressed when changing at the swimming baths, but not in the classroom or at the park.

Case Study 2: Key Stage 2

Children in a mixed Year 5/6 class have been exploring the ways in which all people are different and special. Their focus has been on developing an understanding that being different from one another is not a negative thing, but rather that we are all different, special and unique and in fact difference is the norm.

Using the picture book *Are you a boy or are you a girl?* (Savage and Fisher, 2017) the children have discussed the story of Tiny, who has just moved house because dad has a new job. Tiny explains a range of interests, including dressing up, playing pirates and doctors, and visiting the park. When Tiny starts school a range of experience are encountered relating to gender stereotypes in sport, jobs and activities. The book concludes with Tiny asserting 'I am me!' when questioned about gender identity.

The book includes a range of questions to prompt discussion with readers, which their teacher Mia has used during the lessons (Savage and Fisher, 2017) for example:

- Do the children think Tiny is a boy or a girl?
- Does it matter if he is, she is, they are a girl or a boy?
- What would you ask Tiny is you met him/her/they?

The children also discussed the title of the book, which itself focuses on a gender binary:

Simon   Does it matter whether Tiny is a boy or a girl? Isn't the point of the story that Tiny is Tiny?

Amanda   Can't Tiny just be themself without having to answer people's questions?

Simon   Really the book is about Tiny and their interests, hobbies and moving house. Asking whether they are a boy or a girl gets in the way of the story about Tiny.

Paul   But I wouldn't know whether I want to play with Tiny. How would I know if Tiny would join in boys' games or have boys' hobbies?

Amanda   What games are there that are boys' games? My mum says the England women's football team plays way more exciting football than the men ever do. Sports are just sports, they aren't men's or women's sports anymore, just people's sports.

The children develop their discussion to consider what activities in school are gender-focused. The choir welcomes all members, as does the orchestra, the football team and the computer club. Everyone is able to join in on equal terms, and it doesn't matter how they identify in terms of gender. Paul is not sure whether that will change when they move to secondary school, where sport is segregated by gender. Amanda points out that since they moved into Year 5 the boys and girls are getting changed for PE separately, as they are starting to grow up and want some privacy. This leads to a discussion about whether Tiny would get changed with the boys, the girls, have a choice or have their own place to change. The class doesn't come to a conclusion, although Simon suggests that a good solution might be to ask Tiny what they want. 'That is OK,' says Paul, 'but then you are really still asking whether Tiny is a boy or a girl.'

Such a focus on gender binary raises further questions about how schools and other organizations operate. Gender-binary facilities force individuals to misgender themselves or feel invalidated as they have to use facilities that do not align with their gender identity. For gender-diverse learners, this may present a source of confusion, apprehension and discomfort. Consequently, this has a wider impact on the learner's educational experience (Hewston, 2018: 109). Further, it is important to note that, 'For trans and non-binary children and young people having a positive attitude to their own self-concept can be extremely problematic. At times, teachers and parents may become insistent that what a child feels is neither true, nor acceptable' (Mason and

Woolley, 2019: 151). It is important to consider how to develop inclusive classrooms, particularly for aspects of difference that may not readily be visible within a school. Hellen (2009: 97) suggests that:

> Teachers [are] instructed to have a 'dyslexia-friendly' classroom despite the fact that there may be no diagnosed dyslexic children in the class. [Similarly, creating gender-inclusive classrooms will ensure that] any transgendered children will receive the message that their gender identity is not a problem and that they may not need to conceal their gender identity, at least in school.

Hellen's research indicates that 'the majority of transgendered people were aware that they were transgendered well before puberty' (2009: 88). This contrasts with his suggestion that sexual orientation is more likely to become apparent to an individual when they reach puberty. For example, Hellen cites a survey suggesting that 21 per cent of ten year olds were aware of their sexuality, and only 2 per cent had accepted the fact (p. 85); however, 'the majority of non-transgendered boys and girls do not wait until puberty until they begin to adopt gender-specific behaviour' (p. 89). 'This suggests that gender identity develops earlier than an awareness of one's own sexual orientation' (Mason and Woolley, 2019: 186–7).

Mia later extended learning with her Year 5/6 class by using Yasmen Ismail's book *I'm a Girl!* (2015). In this highly energetic and dynamic text a girl tells the reader that although she is meant to be all sugar and spice, she is in fact sweet and sour and 'not a little flower!' Her behaviours and interests regularly mean that she is mistaken for a boy, and she has to repeatedly correct people's mislabelling. The book concludes when she meets a boy who has to regularly remind people that he is a boy. 'It seems that the two of them are happy with their gender identity, but not the accompanying stereotypes that the world continually puts on them' (Morris and Woolley, 2017: 69).

This provided the opportunity for children to consider their understanding of gendered identities, building on the discussion initiated about Tiny (Savage and Fisher, 2017). In this case, children with very clear binary identities are the focus of discussion, but these are binary identities that challenge traditional gendered stereotypes. Mia asks the children to start to develop 'mood boards' collecting images, colours, textures and any other items they choose to represent who they are. She encourages them to think about their likes, hobbies, friendships and feelings. The development of these very tactile artefacts enables her to emphasize that who we are is represented through all our senses. She explains that who we are can sometimes be seen by others, but also we have thoughts and ideas that sometimes we keep to ourselves and they are also an important aspect of our selves. Amanda reflected:

> I designed my mood board in three dimensions, using layers so that some parts of me were very visible, like the fact that I love to play sports and can be quite loud at times, but other parts of me like my interest in castles were not so visible, as not many friends at school know that I love to read about castles and I enjoy visiting them at the weekend with my mum.

This provided an activity that children could engage with at a range of levels, with some, like Amanda, developing a layered and relatively complex representation of themselves, whilst others engaged in more practical ways appropriate for their stage of development or maturity.

This case study addresses the objectives for *Relationships and Sex Education*, namely that by the end of primary school children should know:

> the importance of respecting others, even when they are very different from them (for example, physically, in character, personality or backgrounds), or make different choices or have different preferences or beliefs.
>
> DfE, 2019: 21

and

> that in school and in wider society they can expect to be treated with respect by others, and that in turn they should show due respect to others . . .
>
> DfE, 2019: 21

Reflection

Reflecting on the issues raised in the Key stage 2 case study, consider:

- How might you discuss gender identity with children in an open way that allows the way in which they identify to be valued?
- Would the use of high-quality picture books enable you to introduce diversity into the classroom that is not otherwise visible? Might there be other strategies you could use?
- Can fictional characters provide a helpful distancing technique to support discussion without personalizing the focus?
- How important is it to indicate that sometimes labels change over time, and how we identify at different points in life may change for some people, as well as remaining constant for others?

Points to consider and conclusion

This chapter has identified a range of strategies to use when tackling controversial issues in the primary school classroom. It is important to acknowledge that we will not all get it right all of the time, at times we will need to ask for advice and help, and on occasion we may need to draw on the expertise of others, on those from outside our school or setting and people with more varied life experience than our own. This is not an indication of failure or inadequacy.

The chapter has considered using appropriate language, both for our own bodies and the identities of others, facilitating the use of vocabulary in a confident manner that can affirm difference, build confidence and empower children to develop self-respect and self-assurance. Such personal attributes are essential if they are to grow and flourish, confident of who they are, what they believe and what they value. These examples are not exhaustive of the issues that may be faced in classrooms, but they illustrate some of the challenges that educators and learners may face.

Points to consider for your own setting

- Why do you feel issues may sometimes be tricky or controversial?
- Who may you approach for help or advice?
- How can we best support children so they are enabled to learn, think and reflect, forming their own views and identities?

Key reading

- Mason, S. and Woolley, R. (2019), *Relationships and Sex Education 3 – 11: supporting children's development and well-being*, London: Bloomsbury.

Further reading

- *Gendered Intelligence*: a not-for-profit community interest company seeking to increase understanding of diverse gender identity; it works particularly with young trans people aged 8–25 years. Available online: http://genderedintelligence.co.uk/
- *Mermaids*: support for trans and gender-diverse children and young people. Available online: www.mermaidsuk.org.uk/

References

Department for Education (DfE) (2013), *The National Curriculum in England: key stages 1 and 2 framework document,* London: Department for Education.

Department for Education (DfE) (2019), *Relationships Education, Relationships and Sex Education (RSE) and Health Education: statutory guidance for governing bodies, proprietors, head teachers, principals, senior leadership teams, teachers,* London: Department for Education.

Hellen, M. (2009), 'Transgender Children in Schools', *Liminalis: Journal of Sex/ Gender Emancipation and Resistance,* 3: 81–99.

Hewston, R. (2018), 'Gender Diversity', in R. Woolley (ed), *Understanding Inclusion,* 101–13, London: Routledge.

Ismail J. (2015), *I'm a Girl!* London: Bloomsbury.

Mason, S. and Woolley, R. (2019), *Relationships and Sex Education 3 – 11: supporting children's development and well-being,* London: Bloomsbury.

Morris, J. and Woolley, R, eds (2017), *Family Diversities Reading Resource,* 2nd edn, Lincoln: Bishop Grosseteste University and University of Worcester. Available online: https://libguides.bishopg.ac.uk/childrensliterature (accessed 8 September 2019).

NSPCC (2019) *NSPCC: Let's Talk Pants.* Available online: https://www.nspcc.org.uk/preventing-abuse/keeping-children-safe/underwear-rule/ (accessed 8 September 2019).

Saltz, G. (2008), *Amazing You! Getting smart about your private parts.* London: Puffin Books.

Savage, S. and Fisher, F. (2017), *Are you a boy or are you a girl?* London: Jessica Kingsley.

Woolley, R. (2010), *Tackling Controversial Issues in the Primary School: facing life's challenges with your learners,* London: Routledge.

Woolley, R. (ed) (2018), *Understanding Inclusion,* London: Routledge.

Woolley, R. (2020), 'Tackling Controversial Issues in Primary Education: perceptions and experiences of student teachers', *Religions,* 11 (4): 184.

3

Little Learners in a Big World

Lorna Williams

This chapter explores:

- The Early Years Foundation Stage and its links to PSHE and RSE through the early learning goals;
- Ideas and approaches that are appropriate and sensitive to the needs of the youngest learners;
- Examples of innovative practice to support practitioners within a range of early years settings such as nurseries, preschools and schools.

As a prime area of the Early years foundation stage profile (EYFSP) (DfE, 2017), Personal social and emotional development is situated at the heart of early years practice. It forms the core of everyday experiences in early years settings embedding a holistic approach. From the moment little learners are inducted, early years practitioners pride themselves in building strong relationships and open communication with children and families. Supporting the youngest children to feel happy and secure, alongside providing a high-quality PSHE education is vital in equipping young learners with robust foundations on which to build future success. Despite proposed changes to the EYFSP in 2021, Personal social and emotional development will remain a prime area of learning, with suggested early learning goals for 'Self-regulation', 'Managing self' and 'Building relationships'. These early learning goals alongside 'Physical development' and 'Understanding the World' underpin and support the Relationships Education, Relationships and Sex Education (RSE) and Health Education Statutory Guidance (2019) from Year 1 onwards. To support the reader to navigate this chapter, links with this statutory guidance will be indicated below each relevant section.

The Little learner

Knowledge of early child development is fundamental to the early years practitioner, underpinning the principles of good early years practice within settings. Most notably, Bronfenbrenner's ecological system (1979, cited in Doherty and Hughes, 2014: 12–15) highlights the interaction between the internal and external factors on a child's personal, social and emotional development. Approaching PSHE in the early years is vital for the development of children's learning and thinking and so should begin there. The Nutbrown Review (2012: 2) concurs that excellent early educational experiences have the potential to impact on a child's wellbeing, learning and development with far-reaching effects in their present and future life. Congruently, Ofsted's focus on 'cultural capital' in the early years inspection handbook (2019: 31), endorses curriculum design and provision that encapsulates the 'essential knowledge that children need to prepare them for their future success'. In this context, cultural capital refers to the rich experiences that practitioners provide to enable children to flourish and be successful regardless of their starting points. This requires practitioners to have a strong knowledge of the child and their previous experiences, often in collaboration with parents and carers. This understanding supports practitioners to facilitate learning and play experiences, enhancing knowledge and skills and providing next steps to form solid learning foundations. Central to this is the importance of the child themselves, their voice and rights. Fundamentally children need to build positive and trusting relationships, which encourage open communication and confidence that their voice will be heard, valued and respected by the adults in their lives (UNICEF, 1990).

Inducting little learners

Whether inducting little learners to Preschool or Reception, many settings begin with 'I am unique' or 'Marvellous Me' topics, supporting children to gain confidence and a sense of self-identity within the group. Activities often focus on the child's family and life experiences, embedding the early learning goals of 'Personal social and emotional development', as well as 'Physical development' through healthy eating and self-care. Time is invested in gently introducing children to school rules, positive behaviour, building friendships, social play and teamwork. Induction underpins much of the PSHE and RSE guidance, enabling practitioners to learn and understand the family dynamics through adopting a triangulated approach; building strong parental–pupil–practitioner relationships. Often this process begins in the term prior to the child's induction to Preschool or Reception with home visits, stay and play sessions, open evenings and induction meetings. Home visits provide opportunities for practitioners to gain insight into the little learner, their family dynamics and are an effective way to begin to build strong relationships. I recall many fond memories of dancing with twins in their kitchen, hunting for a snake in the garden (thankfully the stuffed variety) and rustling through a playroom dressing-up box to find a far from flattering outfit! Equally, the early experiences of a new setting are critical in supporting the child and family with any new transition. The first days and weeks with unfamiliar adults can be traumatic for both children and carers. Bowlby's attachment theory (1958, cited in Doherty and Hughes, 2014: 47) resonated with me throughout my practice, particularly when inducting little learners. Acknowledging and respecting these emotions is important for the child – in that moment they are feeling upset, insecure, unsettled and anxious. Kindness, patience and understanding are qualities that the early years practitioner needs in abundance. Consider the enabling environment by providing a quieter space, such as a cosy corner or den, where a child can quietly reflect or be comforted and supported by a practitioner. This quiet reflective space may also be vitally important to a child with special education needs and disabilities (SEND) or English as an additional language (EAL), ensuring that the setting is inclusive to a diverse range of needs. When supporting little learners in these early days of induction, practitioners should seek to facilitate opportunities for children to interact through play, build positive relationships and support their confidence to communicate. Further strategies that support children during induction could involve a 'special things basket' in which children place a comforting item from home to access throughout the day. Visual timetables and social stories can be an effective way to support children to settle to unfamiliar routines. It has long been recognized according to Maslow's hierarchy of needs (1943, cited in Beckley, 2013: 60) that without a child feeling emotionally secure with their basic needs being met, little learning can occur. Ultimately, successful induction results in happy, safe and engaged little learners. What better way to engage and value the little learner than celebrating their amazing and unique family? The first case study will reflect upon an early years' friendly approach to diverse families and the importance of loving families.

Case Study 1: Example from practice

Tara works in a Preschool setting, working with small focused groups over the course of each morning.

I wanted to explore the concept of family in its many different forms with three and four year olds. Using a book as a hook is a lovely route into what may be for some children a very complex concept. Todd Parr's 'The Family Book' (2010) is a delightfully gentle way of involving young children in conversations around their family dynamics but also introducing them to family diversity through exploring what makes families unique as well as similar. As a group, we began by sharing the story and talking about the different families depicted in the story. I then provided a range of upcycled ornate photograph frames and paper so that the children could draw their family portraits. I did not stipulate who they should include but simply said draw your family. Naturally, there were stepbrothers and sisters, uncles, aunts, grannies, grandpa's, cats, dogs and even a pet lizard! Some children chose to depict two families within their picture frame. The range of families was diverse but each special in its own unique way. We displayed these portraits within the child's chosen frame in our 'Family Showcase'. The children proudly presented their family to the class. This was a perfect way to get to know the children's family dynamics as seen through their eyes. The 'family' chatter encouraged dialogue about what is special about their family; special events and traditions of family; and commonalities and differences. 'The Family Book' is beautifully illustrated and conveys the simple message that all families love and care for each other no matter what shape, size or form. The children were mesmerized by the bold images and quirky characterization. The text is simple but does not shy away from the diverse world that children live in where families may live far apart or have two daddies or mummies. The great thing about Parr's book is that it allows children to explore concepts that may be beyond their own experience, whilst celebrating inclusivity for those children who are living in diverse families.

Links to Relationships Education, Relationships and Sex Education (RSE) and Health Education Statutory Guidance (2019)

Families and people who care for me:

- that families are important for children growing up because they can give love, security and stability.
- the characteristics of healthy family life, commitment to each other, including in times of difficulty, protection and care for children and other family members, the importance of spending time together and sharing each other's lives.

- that others' families, either in school or in the wider world, sometimes look different from their family, but that they should respect those differences and know that other children's families are also characterised by love and care.
  that stable, caring relationships, which may be of different types, are at the heart of happy families, and are important for children's security as they grow up.

Reflection

Consider the following points:

- Some children may share complex family dynamics – how will you manage this sensitively?
- How will you support all little learners to understand that there are diverse families that may differ from their own?
- What are the key messages that you will convey regarding similarities in loving families?

Healthy little learners

Currently Physical development incorporates 'Health and self-care' as an early learning goal (DfE, 2017). Proposals for the new EYFS framework to be introduced in 2021, place aspects of personal hygiene, personal needs and understanding healthy eating in Personal social and emotional development under the early learning goal 'Managing Self'. Regardless of changes to the documentation in the future of early years education, there is clear underpinning from the Relationships Education, Relationships and Sex Education (RSE) and Health Education Statutory Guidance (2019). For many years now the government has invested in healthy eating with the School Fruit and Vegetable Scheme (SFVS) launched in 2000, entitling four to six year olds in state funded schools to a daily portion of fruit or vegetables (NHS, 2017), and more recently, from September 2014, free school meals for children in Reception, Year 1 and Year 2. In addition, milk is provided for children up to the term in which they are five years old (DfH, no date). These government schemes support overwhelming research surrounding child obesity, as well as evidence that performance in school is affected by how well children are nourished. Practitioners support children to try new foods through shared snack times, which often involve story time or social time peers, creating an enjoyable occasion. We all appreciate that young children will try new experiences in a peer group. Often, a parent worried about a fussy eater is surprised when the practitioner reports that their child tucked into a meal with their friends that in three years the parent has never persuaded them to try! The social aspect of eating is so important. Alongside this, a key role of the early years practitioner is to support young children to become more independent in dressing and undressing for PE; encourage personal hygiene – adopting good hand washing habits; and promoting physical activity as a means to stay healthy. Many local authorities employ health practitioners who will visit settings with what I fondly call the 'glitter bug' (the UV light box that can detect bacteria) and teach children about good hand washing routines. In addition, healthy eating sessions, exploring food groups, making 'sugar swaps' and the 'Eatwell Guide' support even the youngest learners to understand how to care for and nourish their bodies with healthy, balanced diets. Additionally, dental hygienists have children's programmes that can be delivered in settings.

Case Study 2: Example from practice

Luke's Reception class are exploring a 'Happy, Healthy Me' topic.

Wilfred the wolf is unhealthy, feasting on a diet of fizzy drinks, crisps and sweets! He cannot run, climb or jump . . . he cannot even bend down to tie his own shoelaces! Like all wolves his favourite snack is CHILDREN! But alas, he cannot ever catch them because he is so unhealthy. This fabulous story takes children on a journey with Wilfred the Wolf from unhealthy to more healthy habits with the help of the Brownbread family who adopt him and teach him good dental hygiene, the importance of exercise and healthy eating (*The Healthy Wolf* by David Bedford, 2002). I used this story to introduce a 'Happy Healthy Me' topic within my Reception class. The children designed assault courses for Wilfred and then created these using apparatus and challenged one another to complete the course. Healthy eating was explored as a team by creating a healthy lunchbox for Wilfred. Role play is a great way to involve children and as a class we set up a dental surgery, doctors, opticians and even a smoothie bar all to encourage Wilfred Wolf to stay on track with his healthy eating. The children created their own healthy eating posters to display around school and became ambassadors of healthy snacking, opening a healthy tuck shop for Key Stage 2 pupils at break time. A knock-on impact that I had not anticipated was the supportive comments and praise from parents. Many of their children made healthier choices, tried new foods, chose to have a break from screen time to get into the fresh air and be active and even requested and tried new foods. It seems that Wilfred Wolf was a positive role model for the children after all!

Links to Relationships Education, Relationships and Sex Education (RSE) and Health Education Statutory Guidance (2019)

Health and wellbeing

Mental wellbeing:

- the benefits of physical exercise, time outdoors, community participation, voluntary and service-based activity on mental wellbeing and happiness.

Physical Health and Fitness:

- the importance of building regular exercise into daily and weekly routines and how to achieve this; for example, walking or cycling to school, a daily active mile or other forms of regular, vigorous exercise.

Health and Prevention:

- about dental health and the benefits of good oral hygiene and dental flossing, including regular check-ups at the dentist.
- about personal hygiene and germs including bacteria, viruses, how they are spread and treated, and the importance of handwashing.

Reflection

Consider the following points:

- We cannot assume that all little learners will have healthy routines and awareness. How will you sensitively support little learners with health and well-being in your setting?
- How will you adapt your learning environment to encourage and promote healthy eating, self-care routines and physical activity?

Little learners making sense of the big world

The importance and value placed on children making sense of the diverse world around them is seen in the specific area of 'Understanding the world', fostering children's social, cultural and ecological understanding. Looking beyond their own experience to the experiences of others, talking about similarities and differences in other communities, cultures or religions. Sykes (2016: 140, cited in Cox and Sykes, 2016) discusses the importance and challenges surrounding cultural diversity and suggests that understanding family beliefs, traditions and cultures enables children and their families to respect one another. This can be showcased by involving families in learning through: parent pop-ins; celebratory assemblies; and 'marvellous me' – a box that the child fills with special things and shares with the class. Projects that involve fundraising for a cause effectively involve children, families and the wider community. For example, learning about endangered tigers may prompt a 'Toys for Tigers' campaign, enthusing children to donate their old toys and set up a sale for the community, with a view to raising money for adoption fees.

Inclusion can be a difficult concept for young children and approaching this in a fun and imaginative way can help children to consider how it feels to be included regardless of differences in ethnicity, gender or culture. An effective and accessible idea for young children could be to use an alien. Children are responsive to the feelings of the alien who appears in their woodland area one morning. This provokes discussion surrounding feelings of isolation, sadness and loneliness, enabling children to empathize and consider how they can help to make the individual feel welcomed. Rich discussion surrounding diversity and respecting differences can be tackled in a sensitive child-friendly way. Just as a new child would be welcomed, the children quickly embrace, support and help this little alien to feel accepted and part of the group. This project would also enable children to consider the complex bitter-sweet emotion when the alien returns to their home planet – happy to be going home but sad to be saying farewell to new friends.

Links to Relationships Education, Relationships and Sex Education (RSE) and Health Education Statutory Guidance (2019)

Health and wellbeing

Caring friendships:

- how important friendships are in making us feel happy and secure, and how people choose and make friends.
- the characteristics of friendships, including mutual respect, truthfulness, trustworthiness, loyalty, kindness, generosity, trust, sharing interests and experiences and support with problems and difficulties.
- that healthy friendships are positive and welcoming towards others, and do not make others feel lonely or excluded.

Respectful relationships:

- the importance of respecting others, even when they are very different from them (for example, physically, in character, personality or backgrounds), or make different choices or have different preferences or beliefs.
- practical steps they can take in a range of different contexts to improve or support respectful relationships.

Little learners with misconceptions and tricky questions

Often, the world can be a confusing place through the eyes of a three-, four- or five-year-old. We cannot simply wrap children in cotton wool or keep them in a bubble. Ultimately, they will be exposed to the complexities of an adult world where messages can be mixed and confusing. Thankfully, we have moved a long way from the notion that children should be 'seen and not heard'. Greater encouragement for children to communicate feelings and openly ask questions means that we as practitioners can help to demystify, draw connections and unscramble misconceptions. Integral to this is helping children to join the dots in a more coherent manner, whilst still being sensitive to their developing understanding. Throughout my career, I have been asked some probing, obscure and frankly hilarious questions by tiny people. 'Why are zebras striped?', 'How does the sea get inside a shell?', the classic 'Where do babies come from?'. All answers have always been approached with honesty, sensitivity and respect whilst being ultimately aware of not squashing their sense of awe and wonder, often responding, 'I am not sure, shall we find out together?'. Sadly, children are exposed to sadness, loss, hurt and disappointment. However, by being open and honest, using sensitive, age appropriate and clear language we can support, guide and nurture. An example of this was a young child who was suffering the bereavement of a parent – a heart breaking, painful and confusing event. Whilst exploring forest school, this youngster began to talk openly about saying goodbye to the parent but expressed confusion through the question, 'The body will be in a box, where will the head be?' Such a terrifying and literal interpretation through the eyes of a four-year-old trying to make sense of an adult phrase. The candid openness and careful choice of words is so important from adults supporting the youngest children. Parental partnership at such a difficult time is integral to ensuring that as practitioners we support with sensitivity, respect and empathy. This strong practitioner–learner openness can often lead to disclosures from children and naturally in this event, safeguarding procedures should be followed accordingly.

Read more on supporting young children with bereavement: https://www.childbereavementuk.org/supporting-bereaved-children-and-young-people

Read more on safeguarding: https://assets.publishing.service.gov.uk/government/uploads/system/uploads/attachment_data/file/800586/Inspecting_safeguarding_.pdf

Links to Relationships Education, Relationships and Sex Education (RSE) and Health Education Statutory Guidance (2019)

Mental wellbeing:

- that there is a normal range of emotions (e.g. happiness, sadness, anger, fear, surprise, nervousness) and scale of emotions that all humans experience in relation to different experiences and situations.
- how to recognise and talk about their emotions, including having a varied vocabulary of words to use when talking about their own and others' feelings.

Points to consider and conclusion

'Children are like wet cement. Whatever falls on them makes an impression.'

Dr Hiam Ginnot

These words may resonate with the early years practitioner. The impact that practitioners make on the youngest learners can last a lifetime and because of this practitioners must tread with care, thought and compassion. Early years practitioners must ensure that they encourage openness, enquiry and balanced views, whilst not inflicting their own opinions. Vital within this role is preparing children for the ever-changing world. Early years practitioners are role models to the children, families and the wider community. Central to this is the little learner and their holistic development into healthy, happy and secure citizens of tomorrow.

Points to consider for your own setting

- What are the key issues pertinent to your early years setting?
- How do practitioners support transitions for little learners?
- In what ways does your setting plan learning opportunities for children that underpin PSHE and R(S)HE?

Key reading

- Reardon, D. (2018), *Early years teaching and learning*, London: Sage.

Further reading

- Cox, A. and Sykes, G. (2016), *The Multiple Identities of the Reception Teacher: Pedagogy and Purpose*, London: Sage.
- Palaiologou, I. (2016), *The Early years foundation stage: theory and practice*, London: Sage.

References

Bedford, D. (2002), *The Healthy Wolf*, London: Little Tiger Press.

Beckley, P. (2013), *The New Early Years Foundation Stage: Changes, Challenges and Reflections*, Berkshire: Open University Press.

Cox, A. and Sykes, G. (2016), *The Multiple Identities of the Reception Teacher: Pedagogy and Purpose*, London: Sage.

Department for Education (DfE) (2017), *Statutory framework for the early years foundation stage*, London: Department for Education.

Department for Education (2019), *Relationships Education, Relationships and Sex Education (RSE) and Health Education: statutory guidance for governing bodies, proprietors, head teachers, principals, senior leadership teams, teachers*, London: Department for Education.

Department for Health (DfH) (no date), *The Nursery Milk Scheme*. Available online: https://www.nurserymilk.co.uk (accessed 18 September 2019).

Doherty, J. and Hughes, M. (2014), *Child development: theory and practice 0-11*, 2nd edn, Harlow: Pearson.

National Health Service (NHS) (2017), *School fruit and vegetable scheme*. Available online: https://assets.nhs.uk/prod/documents/SFVS-factfile-2017.pdf (accessed: 18 September 2019).

Nutbrown, C. (2012), *Foundations for Quality. The Independent Review of Early Education and Childcare Qualifications, Final Report*, London: DfE.

Ofsted. (2019), *Early years inspection handbook for Ofsted registered provision*, London: Crown.

Parr, T. (2010), *The Family Book*, New York: Hachette Book Group.

UNICEF UK. (1990), *A summary of the un convention on the rights of the child*. Available online: https://downloads.unicef.org.uk/wp-content/uploads/2010/05/UNCRC_summary-1.pdf?_ga=2.167702903.817685369.1568790815-1744847567.1568790815 (accessed 18 September 2019).

4

Picture-perfect Drama

Sharon Lannie

This chapter explores:

- *Why* picturebooks and drama can support the teaching of PSHE and RSE;

- *How* picturebooks and drama can support the teaching of PSHE and RSE;

- Picturebooks and drama strategies which promote key strands of PSHE and RSE.

Above all, [picturebooks] can cultivate the social imagination and help us imagine new possibilities for ourselves and the world.

Wissman, 2019: 19

The above quotation may seem magnanimous, but picturebooks have long been understood to be more than a simple, light-hearted read with very young children. Book awards such as The Carnegie and Kate Greenaway Medals, The Newbery Medal, The Guardian Children's Fiction Prize and The UKLA book awards have raised the profile of picturebooks for children and have asserted the powerful themes and multi-layered meanings within; yes, the storylines and illustrations may be enjoyed at a surface level, but dig deeper and there may be much more to consider. Therefore, picturebooks can be read and understood at different levels by readers from four years old to ninety-four years old (Evans, 1998: xv; Evans, 2015).

Academics have written widely about picturebooks and the role they play in children's early literacy, emotional development, intellectual development and thinking skills (Evans, 1998; Roche, 2015). Through picturebooks, essentially the relationship between text and image, many readers can enhance their understanding of the most complex of social issues, enabling children to 'have the potential to gain a deeper sensitivity to the characters' emotions and intentions, and greater insight into the issues and struggles portrayed in the books, than may be possible when reading the text alone' (Burke and Peterson, 2007: 74). The themes and images in picturebooks mean they are key in providing a visual insight into issues which are instrumental in the Relationships and Sex Education (RSE) framework (DfE, 2019) and PSHE strands (DfE, 2017).

How can drama help?

Alongside picturebooks, drama is key for exploring issues. It has been widely documented that drama offers students an opening to other worlds. Drama provides a context for learning about literacy and exploring new and abstract concepts, even for children who have not learnt to read and write (Brown, 2017). Essentially, through drama:

- Children can take risks;
- Explore other values and lives (safely);
- Explore issues from different perspectives;
- Have a voice outside their own idea of 'self';
- Problem-solve;
- Collaborate.

This is why picturebooks and drama are important; both offer a 'way in' and a 'safe' place to begin this exploration. Key drama strategies mean that issues can be 'addressed through means of reasoned and informed reflection, debate and evaluation' for all ages (Woolley, 2010: 2). Role play, freeze-frame, thought-tapping and conscience alley are all drama techniques that can work alongside picturebooks to explore almost any area within RSE. This chapter aims to look at how you might use a picturebook with drama to explore the key themes in the RSE framework.

The strategies used in this chapter are certainly not new and are already part of many teachers' toolbox. If you want a reminder (or introduction) to what these strategies are, please look at David Farmer's fabulous website: https://dramaresource. com/drama-strategies/

'Controversial' issues through picturebooks and drama

The RSE guidance and PSHE strands ensure that children are exposed to, supported and encouraged to consider such issues with a view to achieving greater tolerance and understanding. Of course, when a subject is not factual or have 'clear answers', teachers may find themselves unsure as to where the conversation may lead or what they 'can or cannot say'. Issues which may be complicated or controversial for some teachers, may not be for others. Wooley (2010) suggests that some teachers (and pupils) may see controversy where others do not; 'almost any issue can feel controversial when people hold different beliefs, views or values' (Woolley, p. 2). Woolley goes on to say that other reasons that issues may be controversial could be because of the subject matter and/or the relevance to the setting or the individual. For example, discussions around healthy eating, normally a 'safe' subject, may feel uncomfortable when a significant number of the class are overweight; death itself may not be controversial, but death caused by terrorist attacks or suicide may be areas which are uncomfortable for teachers to explore.

When are children ready for social issues?

The Cambridge Primary Review (Esmee Fairbain Foundation, 2007) , considered to be the most comprehensive enquiry into education in England, found through research that children as young as four had their own views and concerns around wider social issues. These included issues around climate change, global warming, pollution, terrorism and poverty in other countries. Local issues were also on their mind: 'traffic; the lack of safe play areas, rubbish, graffiti, gangs of older children, knives and guns' (Esmee Fairbain Foundation, p. 12). Children were aware of these issues through their families, friends and the media. With the opportunity, children could develop and enhance their knowledge of issues, from a very young age. Ultimately, teachers know the children in their class and should utilize this knowledge, along with discussion with colleagues and parents, to make decisions which are right for their class.

Reflection

What picturebooks do you already have in your classroom?

Revisit the books in your classroom with an RSE 'hat' on. You may be surprised by how many books you already have which reflect social issues through the key strands. For example, refer back to *Elmer* (McKee, 1989) when talking about differences; remind children of *The Smartest Giant in Town* (Donaldson, 2010) when talking about kindness; *Voices in the Park* (Browne, 2001) for points of view and perspective or *The Journey* (Sana, 2016) for refugees and changing communities.

A quick internet search might bring up a wealth of interesting books relating to a key theme (some have been included at the end of this chapter – see Table 5), but *how* to use that book to explicitly teach issues may be the challenge. The case studies below may support you with this.

Case Study 1: Key Stage 1

Picturebook: Julian is a Mermaid (Love, 2018)

Summary: Julian is on the bus with his Nana and sees three women dressed elaborately as mermaids and is captivated; he is determined to become one. But what will everyone say? A simple story of a boy wanting to be a mermaid offers further discussion around gender stereotypes, identity, family and societal expectations.

Lois added *Julian is a Mermaid* to her Year 2 class reading corner where the children could share and enjoy the book. During reading time, Lois overheard three children (two girls and a boy) as they were sharing the book. They got to the part where it said *'Julian LOVES mermaids'* which shows beautiful illustrations of Julian throwing off his clothes and feeling 'free' as he becomes a mermaid. Whilst looking at the pictures, the children were chatting about the text. At one point, one of the girls said:

'It's a bit weird he likes mermaids because he's a boy.'

Reflection

- What does this comment tell you about the possible attitudes and beliefs of the pupil?
- What could the effect be here on the other children in the group?
- If you were the teacher in this situation, what would you do?

Links to RSE framework

Families and people who care for me:

- that others' families, either in school or in the wider world, sometimes look different from their family, but that they should respect those differences and know that other children's families are also characterized by love and care.

Respectful relationships:

- the importance of respecting others, even when they are very different from them (for example, physically, in character, personality or backgrounds), or make different choices or have different preferences or beliefs.
- what a stereotype is, and how stereotypes can be unfair, negative or destructive.

Caring friendships:

- that healthy friendships are positive and welcoming towards others, and do not make others feel lonely or excluded.

Lois felt she needed to open discussion around gender stereotypes and individuality. Table 4 offers support as to how exploring *Julian is a Mermaid* through drama might support this discussion.

Reflection: Beyond your lesson plan . . .

Your discussion with KS1 children around *Julian is a Mermaid*, based on children's own experiences, may well surpass the primary RSE guidance, automatically making links between gender identity and diversity. Consider the following statement that may arise after reading:

'My cousin is a boy, but he wants to be a girl now.'

How would you manage this statement, ensuring sensitivity whilst also inviting discussion?

Table 4 Exploring *Julian is a Mermaid* through drama

Key questions to ask alongside the text	Possible drama strategies
• Look at the front cover. What does Julian's posture/use of colour in the text tell about the way he feels?	• Ask the children to think of a time they felt proud and happy and share this with their partner. • **Freeze-frame:** Can they adopt a pose in the same way?
• Look at the picture of the 'mermaids' as Julian watches on the bus. How has the illustrator drawn the mermaids? How do they make you feel? • What do you think Julian likes about them? • What do we *know* and what do we *think* we know about Julian? • Is Julian like anyone you know? How?	• In small groups, ask the children to **role play** Julian, Nana and the mermaids. What would they be saying to each other, based on their idea from the story so far? This could also be done by having the image on an iPad and children recording the conversation.
• Look at the picture accompanying the words: 'Nana, I am also a mermaid.' • Why would Julian say this? • How do we know Julian is serious about this? • What do the images tell you about how each character is feeling/what they are thinking? • *Why* do you think they are feeling this way?	• **Rumours:** Ask several children to take the part of Julian whilst the rest of the class play his classmates. The teacher should then say the line 'I heard Julian tell his Nana that he is a mermaid.' • Whilst the 'Julians' circulate around the class listening in, the children tell each other gossip/rumours about that line. • The 'Julians' should then feedback what they heard. • Reflect on the positive/negative comments that were heard and the feelings they might produce for Julian.

• Look at the picture where Nana offers Julian a necklace, accompanying the words:
   'For me, Nana?'
   'For you, Julian?'
• Why does Nana give Julian the necklace?
• Are you surprised by Nana's actions?
• What might she have done/said?
	• **Hot seat** with the teacher in role as Nana. The children should ask Nana questions about her thoughts and feelings on Julian's love of mermaids.
	• The teacher might direct questions or answers to provoke discussion, clarify or reassure. for example:
	   At first, I didn't understand . . .
	   I am so happy when Julian is happy . . .
	   What will everyone say . . .

• Think about the book. Ask whether the book would be the same if Julian was a female character. Why?	
• Should Julian stop being a mermaid? Would it be better/worse if he did? • Can you think of other stories where people are different?	• **Conscience alley:** Julian is happiest as a mermaid. Ask the children to give Julian their advice as he passes through.

Case Study 2: Key Stage 2

Picturebook: *The Promise* (Davies, 2013)

Summary: At its most simple, this picturebook tells the story of a young thief who reforms after unwittingly making a promise to a victim. However, this multi-layered book offers the opportunity to explore the effect of poverty and the impact of the environment on its community. The use of illustrations and colour reflect the mood of the book and the language is emotive.

Without revealing the book, Daniel shared a picture from *The Promise* with his Year 4 class. The picture depicted a huddle of sketched, blandly-coloured characters huddled together. One character (a girl?) has a hand inside her neighbour's pocket, seemingly about to take something. Daniel gave his class some prompts to consider and asked them to discuss in small groups their impressions of the picture.

Prompts for discussion:

- Talk about what you can *see* in the picture.
- How do the colours used by the illustrator make you feel?
- What impression do you get of the characters?
- What might the characters be saying or thinking?

The children's responses were insightful; discussion around the characters ranged from them feeling 'sad' to 'despondent'; one child described the characters as 'empty' due to the lack of detail in the drawing whilst another said the colours made them think of 'watery mud' and feel 'depressed'. Interestingly, the child with the hand in the pocket divided opinion about whether it was theft or not. In fact, one child was determined it could not be theft as in their view there didn't seem to be anything to take. They all used the pronoun 'he' about this character without question.

Daniel asked the class to spread out into a space and imagine they were one of the people in that picture. He asked them to adopt a pose like any one of the characters in the image, showing sadness, despair and desolation. He asked them to think about what their character might be thinking at that point, bearing their discussions in mind. They were asked to freeze into that position (freeze-frame). Daniel then used the 'thought-tapping' (or 'thought-tracking') strategy as he walked around the room, encouraging the child to share their brief thoughts in role. In role, children shared their perceived feelings as to why the characters might be feeling as they do. Their idea ranged from being cold, bored, getting divorced, falling out with the neighbours, kids getting on their nerves and being poor. Some children adopted a new voice too.

Daniel then revealed the words accompanying the picture: 'I lived by stealing from those who had almost as little as I did. My heart was as shrivelled as the dead trees in the park' (Davies, 2013: 6).

Knowing the character was indeed a thief with a 'shrivelled heart' invited further discussion from the children, and in some cases outrage that one of their community was stealing. They were asked to talk in pairs about the words and pictures using the following prompts:

- Why is the character stealing?
- What can you work out about where they live?

Using a 'conscience alley', the children were asked to line up in two lines facing each other. In role as their previous character, they were to say what they thought to the thief, as the teacher walked past them. Most of the comments were angry and vilified the thief; 'how dare you steal from us'/'get your own stuff'. Some, however, did demonstrate empathy 'why don't you ask for help – you are just a child'.

Daniel was able to take some of these responses to open further class discussion; it hadn't been planned, but Daniel took the opportunity to explore the issue of 'is it ever right to steal?' Keen to allow everyone to take part, he used a 'line of continuum' where all pupils stood reflecting whether they 'strongly agreed' or 'strongly disagreed' that 'people who steal are bad'. The visual result of forming a line meant that all children were able to see what everyone thought and could respond to ideas from others. Some children began to move themselves around the line as they heard and considered other children's responses.

The class then shared the story, focusing on the character's own transformation and the effect of the environment on the community.

Daniel divided the class into small groups and gave them a scenario to role play in groups:

1 You are the local councillors having a meeting – you want to improve the area and you have some money to do this. Role play the meeting deciding what you want to do to the area to improve it. (3–5 pupils)
2 You are a group of children from the community planning what you are going to do that night. You decide what your environment is like and how that helps you decide what to do. (3–5 pupils)
3 The reformed character in the story is now grown up and married with children. You are playing the part of a member of that family and are asking what they were like as a child. What will you ask/ tell? (3–5 pupils)
4 You are a television crew making a programme about the character in the book and how they changed their life. Interview him/her and people from the community. (3–7 pupils)
5 You are with the old lady who wanted the promise at the beginning of the story. Imagine she goes home to her family the day she has been attacked by the reformed character. What would the conversation be? (2–5 pupils)

Reflection: What was the impact from Daniel's lesson?

Although originally chosen to explore the issues of right and wrong within the community, by allowing the children to engage through another voice, in role, meant that Daniel was able to delve into other themes. The children were encouraged to problem-solve and look beyond the simple 'right' and 'wrong'. Discussions arose around what help and support a child could access; the principles of making change; rehabilitation; crime and punishment; how to keep yourself safe in your community; pre-conceptions around crime and gender and regeneration of local areas.

Links to RSE framework

Mental wellbeing

Pupils should know:

- that there is a normal range of emotions (e.g. happiness, sadness, anger, fear, surprise, nervousness) and scale of emotions that all humans experience in relation to different experiences and situations.
- the benefits of physical exercise, time outdoors, community participation, voluntary and service-based activity on mental wellbeing and happiness.
- simple self-care techniques, including the importance of rest, time spent with friends and family and the benefits of hobbies and interests.

Respectful relationships

Pupils should know:

- that in school and in wider society they can expect to be treated with respect by others, and that in turn they should show due respect to others, including those in positions of authority.

Points to consider for your own setting

- What are the key issues pertinent to your school?
- Do staff have access to a range of inclusive books they can use as a starting point/focus/follow-up for the issue?
- Are children guided/supported through looking at the world from other perspectives – not just their own?

The table below suggests just a few picturebooks which can be used for drama. They have been organized within the PSHE framework to support you with your planning.

Table 5 Suggested picturebooks for use in drama

Health and wellbeing

Harris finds his feet Catherine Rayner	Realizing your talents Not liking parts of your body Grandparents growing old
Perfectly Norman Tom Percival	Being different Being scared about being different Keeping secrets What will people think?
The Whales' Song Dylan Sheldon and Gary Blythe	Different opinions
Something Else Katherine Cave and Chris Riddell	Not belonging Being different
David's World: A picturebook about living with autism Dagmar H. Mueller	Living with autism from a brother's perspective

Relationships

The Bear, the piano, the dog and the fiddle David Litchfield	Great for friendship/jealousy
David's World: A picturebook about living with autism Dagmar H. Mueller	Living with autism from a brother's perspective
Billy Back to Front Sam McCullen	Being different
Donovan's Big Day Lesléa Newman	Same sex marriages.
Footpath Flowers Jon Arno Lawson	Kindness; beauty of our surroundings; parental relationships

Health and wellbeing

Sunday Chutney Aaron Blabey	Being new; establishing identity

Living in the Wider World

Every Child a Song Nicola Davies and Marc Martin	Exploring the rights of the child
Wolves Emily Gravett	Being aware of dangers around you
Zoo Anthony Browne	Zoos/captivity/relationships with parents
The Silence Seeker Ben Morley	Asylum seekers and refugees
My name is not Refugee Kate Milner	Refugees from a child's point of view
Tango Makes Three Justin Richardson	Same sex families
Sam and Dave Dig a Hole Mac Barnett and Jon Klassen	Resilience
10,000 Dresses Marcus Ewert	Gender identity
Webster's Friend Hannah Whaley	Online safety

Key reading

- McDonald, R. (2017), *The Really Useful Drama Book: Using Picture books to Inspire Imaginative Drama*, 1st edn, Oxon: Routledge.
- Wissman, K. (2019), 'Embracing the Power of Picturebooks to Cultivate the Social Imagination', *Bookbird: A Journal of International Children's Literature*, 57 (1): 14–25.

Further reading

The following websites will save you time 'searching' for relevant books and may provide you with ideas to add to your reading list:

- An inclusive reading list: http://www.welcomingschools.org/resources/books/diverse-families/
- Book lists by themes The Family Diversity Reading Resource: http://eprints.worc.ac.uk/5921/1/FDRR.pdf
- A humane book list available online at: https://humaneeducation.org/blog/2018/19-lists-of-childrens-picture-books-for-your-humane-education-classroom/

References

Brown, V. (2017), 'Drama as a valuable learning medium in early childhood', *Arts Education Policy Review*, 118 (3): 164–71.

Burke, A. and Peterson, S.S. (2007), 'A multidisciplinary approach to literacy through picture books and drama', *English Journal*, 96 (3): 74–9.

Davies, N. (2013), *The Promise*, London: Walker Books.

Department for Education (DfE) (2017), *Programme of Study for PSHE Education (Key stage 1-5)*. Available online: https://www.pshe-association.org.uk/curriculum-and-resources/resources/programme-study-pshe-education-key-stages-1%E2%80%935 (accessed 5 September 2019).

Department for Education (DfE) (2019), *Relationships Education, Relationships and Sex Education (RSE) and Health Education: statutory guidance for governing bodies, proprietors, head teachers, principals, senior leadership teams, teachers*, London: Department for Education.

Esmee Fairbain Foundation, U. O. (2007), *The Primary Review: Community Findings*. Cambridge: University of Cambridge.

Evans, J. (1998), *What's in the picture?* 1st edn, London: Sage.

Evans, J. (2015), *Challenging and Controversial Picturebooks: Creative and Critical Responses to Visual Texts*, Oxon: Routledge.

Love, J. (2018), *Julian is a Mermaid*, London: Walker.

Roche, M. (2015), *Developing children's critical thinking through picturebooks: a guide for primary and early years students and teachers*, Oxon: Routledge.

Wissman, K. (2019), 'Embracing the Power of Picturebooks to Cultivate the Social Imagination', *Bookbird: A Journal of International Children's Literature*, 57 (1): 14–25.

Woolley, R. (2010), *Tackling Controversial Issues in the Primary School*, 1st edn, Oxon: Routledge.

5

Developing the 'E' in PSHE

Ben Shakespeare

This chapter explores:

- Some of the key features of economic education;

- How economic education can help ensure the children in your school have the opportunity to develop key life skills in ways which also meet their individual needs;

- How your school can help children develop financial literacy using discussion activities, games and projects linked to key mathematical skills and concepts.

The chapter title may have raised some interesting questions in your head already – what *does* the E actually stand for in PSHE? The national organization, the PSHE Association, outlines that PSHE is focused on supporting children's learning in relation to personal, social, heath and economic education. This aim is also supported by recently published government materials. However, most of the teachers I spoke to whilst writing this chapter, ranging from newly qualified teachers to experienced teachers, associated 'PSHE' with Personal, Social and Health *Education*. This is understandable given other subjects in the curriculum – consider the 'E' in PE or RE, for example. However, the potential lack of awareness regarding the place of economic education is concerning, particularly given recent studies which have shown that adult financial literacy levels in England and Northern Ireland are lower than many other developed countries (OECD, 2017; Aditi Bhutoria, Jerrim and Vignoles, 2018). Financial literacy is a term used by many international organizations (such as the OECD) and governments to refer to a person's level of financial understanding (the UK government chooses to use the term 'financial capability').

> Financial literacy is a combination of awareness, knowledge, skill, attitude and behaviour necessary to make sound financial decisions and ultimately achieve individual financial well-being.
>
> *Atkinson and Messy, 2012: 14*

There are many definitions of financial literacy but Atkinson and Messy provide a useful, holistic definition for us which helps to highlight that any economic education should also focus on developing healthy attitudes and behaviours towards money and finances. Some may argue that this is not on the curriculum and therefore schools should not be expected to teach this content. However, as any teacher of primary children will tell you, a great deal of time is spent helping children to develop their interpersonal skills, helping them to be able to function socially. This is not part of the statutory National Curriculum either, but if school is considered an important place to gain these skills, surely it is an important place to help children become more financially literate too? It is also important to note that mathematics is *not* the same as economic education. However, as this chapter will demonstrate, mathematics provides us with an important opportunity to develop some key skills which can be extremely useful for supporting children as part of economic education, helping them to become financially literate citizens of the future.

Economic education: background and current context

Economic education is not a new idea by any means. It was included as one of the key outcomes of the Every Child Matters agenda, published in 2004 by the then named Department for Children, Schools and Families. This was also supported by the Children Act 2004 and it is important to remember that although the Every Child Matters agenda was archived in 2011 and no longer receives the focus it once did, the Act it built upon obviously still remains in place. Since then, perhaps partly in response to the UK recession in 2008, there have been a string of recommendations calling for economic education to form a statutory part of primary education. In 2011, Ofsted published a report focused on what they referred to at the time as 'economics, business and enterprise education'. In the report, based on school inspection findings, Ofsted emphasized the importance of 'well-planned provision' relating to economic education at 'all key stages' (Ofsted, 2011: 8). Furthermore, in 2013, Ofsted published a review of PSHE education. The report's title, 'Not Good Enough' speaks volumes in itself. The report summarized that in many of the schools visited, 'work on developing pupils' economic wellbeing and financial capability is insufficient' (Ofsted, 2013: 29). The report's findings are unsurprising given the fact that economic education had not been given the curriculum focus needed for schools to prioritize this aspect. As a result of some of these recommendations, in 2014, the newly published secondary National Curriculum (DfE, 2014) included economic education within the programmes of study for 'Citizenship'. For the first time, this ensured that economic education was statutory in secondary schools. It was widely believed that economic education would also form part of the 2014 primary National Curriculum for mathematics (Goddard, Smith and Boycott, 2013). This did not happen and there is still currently no statutory requirement for economic education to be taught to primary-aged children in England.

Since then, there have been many calls for economic education's inclusion within the statutory programmes of study of the primary National Curriculum. In 2016, an All-Party Parliamentary Group (APPG) described this as a 'critical issue' for English schools with a recommendation to 'start younger', particularly given the fact that economic education forms part of the statutory primary curricula in Scotland, Wales and Northern Ireland (APPG, 2016: 7). Most recently, in 2019, another APPG report reiterated the recommendation to make economic education statutory in primary schools (APPG, 2019). A recent international study conducted by UCL and the University of Cambridge adds further weight to these recommendations (Aditi Bhutoria, Jerrim and Vignoles, 2018). This used data from the Organisation for Economic Co-operation and Development (OECD, 2017), gathered from thirty-one different countries, and found that many of the adults surveyed struggled to answer basic questions that were deemed to be indicators of financial literacy.

Reflection

Here are two examples of the questions asked by the OECD during their international survey. After analysis, it was found that one in three adults in England were unable to answer these questions correctly:

1 Suppose, upon your trip to the grocery store you purchase four types of tea packs: Chamomile Tea (£4.60), Green Tea (£4.15), Black Tea (£3.35) and Lemon Tea (£1.80). If you paid for all these items with a £20 note, how much change would you get?
2 Suppose, a litre of cola costs $3.15. If you buy one-third of a litre of cola, how much will you pay?

Consider the implications of this within everyday life and the ability to manage money effectively and confidently.

Now consider the people in your school community (children, parents/carers and staff). How many would be able to answer these questions? What kind of provision does your school make for children to regularly develop the skills needed to answer these types of questions?

The apparent lack of government focus on economic education within primary schools has been further emphasized by the recent move to make only some of elements of the PSHE curriculum statutory from 2020, ignoring the important role that economic education has to play in preparing our children with key life skills. This has caused some concerns, leading the PSHE Association to address this within their response to the government plans. They note 'learning about economic wellbeing is vital' and 'inextricably linked to health and relationships' and that despite its non-statutory status, schools should continue to integrate economic education within their school curriculum (PSHE Association, 2019).

That being said, economic education goes far beyond the mathematical problems posed in the examples taken from the OECD survey. As mentioned earlier, it is important to also focus on the attitudes and behaviours related to financial matters. The attitudes and emotions linked to money – how it feels to have it; spend it; and save it, should be a key part of any school's approach to economic education. Case Study 1, and the Reflection point that follows, provides some examples which consider the wider knowledge, skills and attitudes fundamental to a holistic economic education.

Case Study 1: EYFS and Key Stage 1

This activity has been successfully used with children across EYFS and KS1. It could also be equally applicable to children in KS2. The way in which the activity is presented can be changed to suit the children in your school; the important thing is the discussion that arises and how this discussion is managed sensitively.

Needs and Wants

This is a rich activity which can promote lots of interesting discussion. It can be completed as a simple card-sorting activity too, but this version of the activity can also provide a vehicle to consider the importance of saving.

Children work in pairs and are given a 'game board' with labelled pictures of different items. Although not labelled as such, these items include a mixture of things people *need* to live (clean water, nutritious food and shelter) and other items that people might *want*. Here is an example:

Children are given counters (or coins) to represent the cost of these items and they are then allowed to choose what to buy. The children must keep a running total of their spend, therefore providing a good opportunity for them to practise addition facts too. The size and number of choices on this gameboard can be changed to match the age and needs of your class, the example given is not a definitive version by any means. For example, it could be adapted for older children by labelling items with amounts of money, reflecting the types of calculation expected for that age.

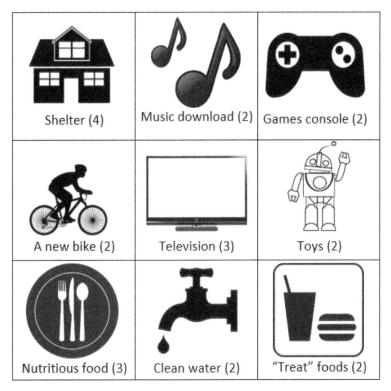

Shelter (4)	Music download (2)	Games console (2)
A new bike (2)	Television (3)	Toys (2)
Nutritious food (3)	Clean water (2)	"Treat" foods (2)

Figure 3 An example of a 'Needs and Wants' gameboard.

When introducing this activity to a class, I have found that opportunities for discussion (and the all-important learning) are greater when children have the chance to just engage with the resource, rather than providing too much guidance during the initial teacher explanation. In the example given, the children are given ten counters, with the item 'costs' listed to reflect this. Notice how the 'needs' (shelter, clean water and nutritious food) create a total of nine. The one remaining counter is not enough to buy any of the other items. This limitation can create some interesting responses from the children. For example, I have found that children will often choose to buy a games console and a television but without a home to actually plug it in! They will also often forget that they need clean drinking water to be able to survive! The important point to note here is that the teacher should prompt with questions, rather than 'tell' the children what to do. It is important that children start to reach an understanding regarding the differences between needs and wants through their interactions. For example, try prompting the children by asking them what could be done with the one counter that remains. This can lead to some excellent work on the importance of saving – emphasizing a 'spend a little, save a little' mindset.

Towards the end of the activity, facilitate a whole-class discussion and highlight some of the key learning that has taken place:

- The difference between a 'want' and a 'need'.
- That the things we need (and want) cost money and we must make choices about what to buy.
- That sometimes we do not have all the money needed for some of our 'wants' – we can choose to save up our money for some of these things.
- That some people may not always have the money available to buy everything that they need.

The last point on this list needs to be managed sensitively, but it is an important point to raise. Consider the issue of sensitivity in the following reflection.

Reflection

'Where does money come from?'

This is a really interesting question to ask children – try it, you might be surprised with what they say! Often children have responded to this question by saying things like 'It comes from the wall [cashpoint]', 'the bank' or 'my mummy/daddy's card'. Prompt further discussion by asking how it gets in the bank and many young children simply do not know. Some will show an understanding of the relationship between work and getting paid. This can lead onto discussion about having a job and earning money.

Consider the following points:

- Some children will mention earning (or being given) pocket money, some will have none at all – how will you manage this sensitively?
- 'My mum/dad doesn't have a job, where does their money come from?' – how do we manage this sensitively without avoiding the opportunity to develop understanding?

It is important to always consider the individuals in your class. In order to have rich discussion but also ensure children's emotional wellbeing is cared for, points of discussion should always be generic and never include specific, named individuals.

Like many aspects of PSHE, content can raise interesting topics of conversation and debate, to this extent economic education is no different. Many teachers I have spoken to recognize the importance of economic education for young children. In fact, a recent survey found that 80 per cent of primary school teachers agree that economic education should be part of the primary curriculum (Opinium on behalf of Prudential, 2018). It is also widely recognized that economic education needs to start earlier on in a child's education. However, deciding on the content to be covered can be a contentious issue. Some teachers I have spoken to have expressed concerns causing children to 'worry' about money too early on in their lives. It is important to make clear that economic education is not about getting children to 'worry' about money (although it is important to remember that some children live within an environment where the 'worry' about money is very real indeed). I believe a sensible proposal would be for children to start to the learn the *value* of money from an early age. While it is clear that parents have a responsibility to manage this, schools also have an important part to play.

The importance of early economic education becomes even clearer when we consider research conducted by Whitebread and Bingham (2013). Their research suggests that most children form financial habits by age seven, with both home and school being key influencers in their habit formation. At such a young age we are obviously not expecting children to be able to budget pocket money, but we would want to develop their understanding around the fact that money is not limitless.

The importance of developing children's financial literacy is clear. However, despite some schools incorporating economic education within their school curriculum, having time to do so effectively in an already busy school day can present a key challenge. The approach taken in Case Study 2 is a way of addressing this potential barrier. It makes effective use of curriculum time, combining curriculum subjects together and making meaningful links between them.

Case Study 2: Key Stage 2

This case study outlines an approach taken by some schools to incorporate economic education within real-life projects, providing a sense of purpose and deep learning. As with the previous case study, the ideas explored can be adapted and successfully used within EYFS and KS1.

Class enterprise
In this approach, the class engages with one enterprise activity each term. This involves the children being involved with a plan to make and sell a product in order to raise money. Some schools who have adopted this approach have a different focus for each of the three terms: raising money for charity; raising money for the school; and raising money for the class. An example of a typical enterprise activity is given here.

Enterprise: Raising money for charity – Art and Craft Sale

After discussion, children selected a charity to raise funds for. Children could nominate some local and national charities, giving a brief presentation to the rest of the class as to why a particular charity should be supported. A class vote then took place and it was decided to raise funds for a local charity which helped to train dogs for people who were blind and partially sighted. The class wrote to the local charity and they offered to come in to explain more about their work, the costs involved and how they use donations.

Children then worked in groups to generate ideas for what they could produce and sell in order to make money. Recent topic work across Design and Technology and Art inspired the children to open a Christmas crafts shop and work quickly began on selecting items for sale.

The cost of producing each item was calculated by the children, using school supply catalogues, and then items were chosen based on the ease of producing these items and the profit they would generate. After the 'products' were made, the children turned the classroom into a craft shop and sold the items they had made. Although supported by the teacher, children were expected to take ownership of managing the finances; giving correct change and totalling up their 'till' at the end of business.

Consider some of the opportunities for learning within this example of class enterprise:

- Developing an understanding that items have a cost to produce and that in order to make a profit, we need to consider the price of an item.
- That money can be earned in exchange for work and effort.
- Solving mathematical problems in a real context.

Although the final point is a statutory part of the primary National Curriculum for England, class enterprise enables children to solve these problems using realistic amounts of money and for a real purpose rather than some of the contrived 'real-life' contexts which are often given to children.

Another benefit of this approach is that it can help to highlight the importance of economic education to the wider school community, encouraging families to continue these discussions with their children. The link between home, school and economic education has been highlighted as particularly 'powerful' in developing children's financial literacy (APPG, 2016: 38) and therefore should be encouraged in any school's approach to economic education.

Points to consider and conclusion

This chapter has explored a range of issues surrounding economic education. Some of the key arguments and related research have been outlined to help illustrate the importance of enabling the children in our care to become more financially literate and confident. As the curriculum currently stands, children in England have no statutory right to economic education, yet all will be expected to be able to function in a world where finances are part of our everyday lives. It is hoped that this chapter encourages you to consider your school curriculum and the extent to which it really supports these aims.

It is unclear whether or not the current statutory curriculum requirements will change in the future. The Money Advice Service, an independent organization set up by the UK Government, has continued to include a focus on economic education within primary schools as part of their UK-wide 'Financial Capability' strategy (Financial Capability, 2015: 32). Alongside this, they plan to support schools in appointing a 'financial education lead' in order to help prioritize economic education within schools. It will be interesting to see if these plans ever come to fruition. Regardless of this, children deserve an education which helps them to develop the skills they require in order to have the potential to live a financially healthy life and it is clear that schools, as well as families, will need to take an active role in this.

Points to consider for your own setting

- To what extent does your school curriculum support economic education?
- How will your school ensure a holistic approach to economic education, also focusing on the behaviours and attitudes related to money?
- All schools are required to teach children to solve problems involving money, as part of the primary mathematics curriculum. However, as discussed in this chapter, this does not encapsulate a holistic view of financial literacy – to what extent do your children have chance to engage with truly 'real-life' contexts and problems?

Key reading and resources

- Young Enterprise Planning Frameworks – free tools to help you map out objectives, also considering behaviours and attitudes towards money. Available online: https://www.young-enterprise.org.uk/teachers-hub/financial-education/resources-hub/financial-education-planning-frameworks/
- Cha-ching – free lesson plans and video resources (this website has been awarded the Financial Education Quality mark by Young Money/pfeg). Available online: https://www.cha-chingeducation.co.uk/
- My Money Week – held each year since 2009, lots of resources and planning. Available online: https://www.young-enterprise.org.uk/teachers-hub/financial-education/financial-education-programmes/my-money-week/
- My Money Primary Toolkit (2009) available in the National Archives. Available online: https://webarchive.nationalarchives.gov.uk/20120106144053/https://www.education.gov.uk/publications/standard/publicationDetail/Page1/MM-PRI-TKT
- Global Money Week – teaching materials start from age ten. (but could be adapted). Available online: https://globalmoneyweek.org/

References

Aditi Bhutoria, A., Jerrim, J. and Vignoles, A (2018), *The financial skills of adults across the world. New estimates from PIAAC (Working Report).* Available online: https://johnjerrim.com/piaac/ (accessed 5 September 2019).

All-Party Parliamentary Group (APPG) (2016), *Financial Education in Schools: Two Years On – Job Done?,* Available online: https://www.young-enterprise.org.uk/wp-content/uploads/2019/02/APPG-on-Financial-Education-for-Young-People-Final-Report-May-2016.pdf (accessed 5 September 2019).

All-Party Parliamentary Group (APPG) (2019), *Care to talk about Money? The Importance of Financial Education for Children in Care.* Available online: https://www.young-enterprise.org.uk/wp-content/uploads/2019/07/APPG-Fin-Ed-for-children-in-care-2019.pdf (accessed 5 September 2019).

Atkinson, A. and Messy, F-A. (2012), 'Measuring Financial Literacy: Results of the OECD / International Network on Financial Education (INFE) Pilot Study', OECD Working Papers on Finance, Insurance and Private Pensions, No. 15, OECD Publishing. Available online: http://dx.doi.org/10.1787/5k9csfs90fr4-en (accessed 1 September 2019).

DCSF (2003), *Every Child Matters.* Available online: https://assets.publishing.service.gov.uk/government/uploads/system/uploads/attachment_data/file/272064/5860.pdf (accessed 3 September 2019).

Department for Education (DfE) (2014), *National Curriculum in England: Framework for Key Stages 1 – 4.* Available online: https://www.gov.uk/government/publications/national-curriculum-in-england-framework-for-key-stages-1-to-4/the-national-curriculum-in-england-framework-for-key-stages-1-to-4 (accessed 4 September 2019).

Financial Capability (Fincap) (2015), *Financial Capability: Strategy for the UK*. Available online: https://www.fincap.org.uk/en/uk_strategies/uk-strategy (accessed 5 September 2019).

Goddard, G., Smith, V. and Boycott, C. (2013), *PSHE in the Primary School: Principles and Practice,* London: Routledge.

Ofsted (2011) *Economics, business and enterprise education*. Available online: https://www.gov.uk/government/publications/economics-business-and-enterprise-education (accessed 5 September 2019).

Ofsted (2013), *Not yet good enough: personal, social, health and economic education in schools*. Available online: https://assets.publishing.service.gov.uk/government/uploads/system/uploads/attachment_data/file/413178/Not_yet_good_enough_personal__social__health_and_economic_education_in_schools.pdf (accessed 4 September 2019).

Opinium on behalf of Prudential (2018), *Financial Education Not Adding Up for Primary Schools*. Available online: https://www.pru.co.uk/pdf/press-centre/teaching-children-about-money.pdf (accessed 5 September 2019).

PSHE Association (2019), *Government takes 'major step' towards better PSHE for all*. Available online: https://www.pshe-association.org.uk/news/government-takes-%E2%80%98major-step%E2%80%99-towards-better-pshe (accessed 1 September 2019).

The Organisation for Economic Co-operation and Development (OECD) (2017), *G20/OECD INFE report on adult financial literacy in G20 countries*. Available online: https://www.oecd.org/finance/g20-oecd-infe-report-adult-financial-literacy-in-g20-countries.htm (accessed 4 September 2019).

Whitebread, D and Bingham, S. (2013), *Habit Formation and Learning in Young Children*. Available online: https://www.moneyadviceservice.org.uk/en/corporate/habit-formation-and-learning-in-young-children (accessed 2 September 2019).

6

Super Science and the 'Health' in PSHE and R(S)HE

Elena Lengthorn and Rebecca Saunders

This chapter explores:

- How the science national curriculum and the PSHE/R(S)HE curriculum interrelate;
- The use of scientific enquiry in health education;
- How to support pupil progress in working scientifically.

The latest statutory elements of PSHE (including the addition of a compulsory R(S) HE curriculum from September 2020) usher in a new era in recognizing the importance of mandatory teaching on physical health and mental wellbeing, including: personal hygiene; dental health; immunization; active lifestyles; menstruation; and a healthy diet.

Science education has long been a tool to support the delivery of PSHE, with its wonderful opportunities in the exploration of the human body, how it functions and how best to take care of it. The new curriculum obligations provide an opportunity to build 'science capital', widely understood as a conceptual measure of an individual's exposure to and knowledge of science and its relevance to human activities (Langley, 2018), as well as raising their enjoyment levels and attainment in science. There are many connections to be made between science learning and the development of the qualities and skills that our pupils need to thrive, which is the key goal of a PSHE education, a 'curriculum for life' (PSHE Association, 2017).

How much science is actually taking place in the primary classroom? The abolition of the Key Stage 2 SATs for science in May 2009 was an opportunity for science teaching to move beyond 'teaching to the test' and allow time for inspirational science lessons (Hoath, 2019). It appears, unfortunately, to have been de-prioritized with the findings from the 2019 Ofsted report on primary school science concluding:

> Science has clearly been downgraded in some primary schools since the scrapping of the key stage 2 test. This is likely to have a serious impact on the depth and breadth of science understanding and knowledge that pupils take with them into secondary school, which may in turn stifle pupils' later curiosity and interest in the sciences.
>
> Ofsted, 2019

The science opportunities within the PSHE/R(S)HE curriculum allow primary practitioners to build their pupils science capital, a measure of which can be used to help understand how social class affects people's aspirations and involvement in science, which may also help to close the recognized science, technology, engineering and mathematics (STEM) gap (in terms of post-16 uptake of the sciences and creation of suitably qualified science graduates for STEM positions) as research has shown that increased science capital in children leads to them being more likely to follow STEM subjects (Archer, 2015). This is crucial for our planetary future, as well as supporting the personal development of the individual and essential skills for a healthy life.

The vast majority of opportunities to run PSHE/R(S)HE and science complimentary (rather than duplicative) activities are in years 2, 4, 5 and 6. The commonalities have been mapped out on the following matrix.

Hand washing and the spread of disease

It is widely known that children are most at risk from the effects of poor hand hygiene and of 'picking up infections and spreading them to other people' (NHS, 2016). The most recent report on school absenteeism (DfE, 2019a) highlights that absence rates have increased since the previous year and that illness continues to be the main driver for overall absence rates. The PSHE/R(S)HE curriculum gives us the space to address the spread of germs in schools, something that is essential for the health of all our pupils, and indeed the entire school staff, with the most important and straightforward reduction in ill-health coming in the form of hand washing. This is especially relevant in light of our recent global COVID-19 pandemic. 'Enveloped' viruses, such as Coronavirus, have a protective outer layer which soap molecules can dissolve, subsequently killing the virus. This lesson invites pupils to connect with this fundamental hygiene practice through a process of working scientifically.

Working scientifically means using scientific enquiry. The National Curriculum (DfE, 2013) outlines these methods as including observations over time; pattern

Table 6 Commonalities between PSHE/R(S)HE and Science activities

Science National Curriculum Statutory Requirements (DfE, 2013)	Related area of Relationships Education and Health Education Statutory Requirement (from September 2020)	Related area of PSHE curriculum (the H numbers correspond to the PSHE Association Programme of Study 2020)
Year 2 Notice that animals, including humans, have offspring which grow into adults. Find out about and describe the basic needs of animals, including humans, for survival (water, food and air). Describe the importance for humans of exercise, eating the right amounts of different types of food, and hygiene.	About dental health and the benefits of good oral hygiene and dental flossing, including regular check-ups at the dentist. About personal hygiene and germs including bacteria, viruses, how they are spread and treated, and the importance of handwashing. The facts and science relating to allergies, immunization and vaccination.	KS1 H1 – about what keeping healthy means: different ways to keep healthy. KS1 H2 – about foods that support good health and the risks of eating too much sugar. KS1 H3 – about how physical activity helps us to stay healthy; and ways to be physical active everyday. KS1 H5 – simple hygiene routines that can stop germs from spreading. KS1 H7 – about dental care and visiting the dentist; how to brush teeth correctly; food and drink that support dental health. KS1 H26 – about the process of growing from young to old and how people's needs change.
Year 4 Describe the simple functions of the basic parts of the digestive system in humans. Identify the different types of teeth in humans and their simple functions (finding out what damages teeth and how to look after them.)	What constitutes a healthy diet (including understanding calories and other nutritional content). The principles of planning and preparing a range of healthy meals. The characteristics of a poor diet and risks associated with unhealthy eating (including, for example, obesity and tooth decay) and other behaviours (e.g. the impact of alcohol on diet or health).	KS2 H2 – about the elements of a balanced and healthy lifestyle. KS2 H6 – about what constitutes a healthy diet; how to plan meals; benefits to health and wellbeing of eating nutritionally rich foods; risks associated with not teaching a healthy diet including obesity and tooth decay. KS2 H11 – how to maintain good oral hygiene (including correct brushing and flossing); why regular visits to the dentist are essential; the impact of lifestyle choices on dental care.

Science National Curriculum Statutory Requirements (DfE, 2013)	Related area of Relationships Education and Health Education Statutory Requirement (from September 2020)	Related area of PSHE curriculum (the H numbers correspond to the PSHE Association Programme of Study 2020)
Year 5 Describe the differences in the life cycles of a mammal, an amphibian, an insect and a bird. Describe the life process of reproduction in some plants and animals. Describe the changes as humans develop to old age.	Key facts about puberty and the changing adolescent body, particularly from age nine through to age eleven, including physical and emotional changes. About menstrual wellbeing including the key facts about the menstrual cycle.	KS2 H30 – to identify the external genitalia and internal reproductive organs in males and females and how the process of puberty relates to human reproduction. KS2 H32 – about how hygiene routines change during the time of puberty, the importance of keeping clean and how to maintain personal hygiene. KS2 H33 – about the processes of reproduction and birth as part od the human life cycle; how babies are conceived and born (and that there are ways to prevent a baby being made).
Year 6 Recognize the impact of diet, exercise, drugs and lifestyle on the way their bodies function	The risks of an inactive lifestyle (including obesity). The characteristics of poor diet and risks associated with unhealthy eating (including, for example, obesity and tooth decay) and other behaviours (e.g. the impact of alcohol on diet or health). The facts about legal and illegal harmful substances and associated risks, including smoking, alcohol use and drug-taking. The characteristics and mental and physical benefits of an active lifestyle. The importance of building regular exercise into daily and weekly routines and how to achieve this; for example walking or cycling to school, a daily active mile or other forms of regular, vigorous exercise.	KS2 H1 – How to make informed decisions about health. KS2 H2 – about the elements of a balanced, healthy lifestyle. KS2 H3 – about choices that support a healthy lifestyle and recognize what might influence these. KS2 H4 – How to recognize that habits can have both positive and negative effects on a healthy lifestyle. KS2 H7 – how regular exercise benefits mental and physical health; recognize opportunities to be physically active and some of the risks associated with an inactive lifestyle. KS2 H46 – about the risks and effects of legal drugs common to everyday life and their impact on health; recognize that drug use can become a habit which is hard to break. KS2 H47 – to recognize that there are laws surrounding the use of legal drugs and that some drugs are illegal to own, use and give to others.

seeking; identifying, classifying and grouping; comparative and fair testing (controlled investigations); and researching using secondary sources. Pupils should have opportunities to investigate their own answers using data collection, analysis and presentation.

Example Lesson Plan 1

KS1 Lesson Plan – Year 2 – Animals Including Humans

Science Learning Objective: Describe the importance for humans of hygiene and handwashing.

Working Scientifically:

- Asking simple questions and recognizing that they can be answered in different ways.
- Observing closely, using simple equipment.
- Performing simple tests.
- Using their observations and ideas to suggest answers to questions.
- Gathering and recording data to help in answering questions.

PSHE Learning Objective: To learn the importance of, and how to, maintain personal hygiene.

R(S)HE Learning Objectives: to know about personal hygiene and germs including bacteria, how they are spread and treated, and the importance of handwashing.

Resources: bread slices x2, clear sandwich bags, hygiene gloves or tongs, oil, glitter, 4 large washing bowls, soap, hand towel, outlines of hands to record observations or a digital camera.

Key Vocabulary: Hygiene, washing, bacteria, virus, fair test, variable, control.

Health and Safety: Be aware of any gluten allergies. Ensure pupils do not eat the bread or transmit crumbs to their faces. Ensure pupils do not put fingers in mouths during investigation, all pupils need to safely wash hands after experimentation. Ensure that the experiment bags, containing bread, remain sealed for the duration of the investigation.

Introduction: Explain that the children will be thinking like scientists and developing an important skill called *observing*. Explain what this means. Show a slice of bread to the class and tell them that they will start by closely observing this piece of bread. Pass it round from person to person, looking closely at it (make sure they turn it over, feel the texture of it, look at the structure of it – record any adjectives to describe what they can see). Once everyone in the class has handled the bread, take it back and place it in a clear sandwich bag, sealing it thoroughly. Congratulate them on their excellent observation skills!

Remind them that everybody in the class has touched that piece of bread. Would anybody eat it now? Why/why not? Use talk partners to draw out the reasons why it should not be eaten (some people's hands may not have been clean beforehand). Talk about germs/bacteria and what they are.

Explain that we will set up an observation over time to see what happens to the bread after it has been touched by many 'unclean' hands. Draw out predictions from the children – what will they expect the bread to look like after a week or two? Why? Record the pupil predictions and put the bread on display in a safe place in the class and leave. Add pupil predictions to the display. Put another slice of 'clean' bread (using gloves or tongs). Agree a time to regularly check the bread and record observations (drawings/digital photographs).

Activity 1:

Recap prior knowledge of what pupils know about how we keep ourselves healthy. Explore their ideas of how we can we keep ourselves healthy. Discuss how much sleep children need and why, as well as how and why we keep ourselves clean. Discuss illnesses that can be spread. Ask pupils: 'When should we wash our hands?'

Investigation:

What is the best way to remove bacteria from our hands? You could invite pupils to consider how they would investigate this and then provide some options for their consideration:

- Using cold water and no soap;
- Using warm water and no soap;
- Using cold water and soap;
- Using warm water and soap.

Ask the pupils to make predictions and give reasons for their choices. Invite four children to come up and coat their hands in a little oil and then coat them with one teaspoon of glitter (to represent the bacteria which get all over their hands).

Explain that each child is going to carry out one of the variables to see which one is best. How can we keep our test fair? Draw out that they need to all agree to rub their hands at the same speed and for the same length of time, those using soap will need to have the same amount. Carry out the investigation and after a specified time, check their hands for cleanness.

Record the observations on hand outlines or with a digital camera. Which hand-washing conditions were best and why?

Children can write a conclusion answering the question using the data. How did they keep the test fair? Use a writing frame to support, if needed.

Activity 2: Get all the children to wash their hands the 'best' way (as identified by your investigation) and regroup. Take another slice of bread and repeat the starter activity of passing the bread round to each person. Place that piece in a bag and label it as 'Clean Hands'. Add this to the bread display.

Invite children to make predictions about what they think will happen and share their reasoning. Record pupil predictions and add them to the display. These will be referred to at the end of the observation.

Plenary: Draw the class back together and share our findings. Have we answered the question? Explain that bacteria live on our hands all of the time and most of them are harmless. However, some of them can make us ill.

Future Lesson: Return to the bread samples: invite pupils to observe and describe the differences between them. They could revisit their observation skills, drawing sketches of the outcomes and annotating them. Invite pupils to share their reasons for why this has happened and what the impact of it might be. Invite them to extend the investigation by thinking about other conditions that could be investigated. E.g. what would have happened if we had put the bread in the fridge instead? Recap the times when we need to make sure our hands are clean and what might happen if we don't.

Extension ideas: In mixed pairs, devise a handwashing song with actions. Pupils could independently complete a handwashing sequencing activity. Create a poster to inform others when to wash our hands.

Reflection

You could connect your lesson activities to the worldwide advocacy event 'Global Hand Washing Day' (October 15). It's an annual event created by The Global Handwashing Partnership (a group that works to save children's lives and improve health by promoting handwashing with soap), who are dedicated to increasing awareness and understanding about the importance of handwashing with soap as an effective and affordable way to prevent diseases and save lives.

Energy drinks and drugs

At a time when school exclusions for drugs and alcohol have risen by 57 per cent in five years, with an analysis from the Department for Education (DfE, 2019b) showing the highest figure on record for the number of the children permanently excluded from secondary school due to drugs or alcohol (Turner, 2019), it is crucial that we make the most of the opportunity afforded by the PSHE/R(S)HE curriculum to embed education on legal and illegal substances and their associated risks, through the gathering and analysis of scientific data.

Example Lesson Plan 2

KS2 Lesson Plan – Year 6 – Animals Including Humans

Science Learning Objective: To recognize the impact of drugs, alcohol and smoking on the body.

Working Scientifically: Reporting and presenting findings from enquiries (including conclusions, causal relationships and explanations of and a degree of trust in results) in oral and written forms such as displays and other presentations.

PSHE Learning Objective: To learn which, why and how, commonly available substances and drugs (including alcohol, tobacco and 'energy drinks') can damage their immediate and future health and safety; that some are restricted and some are illegal to own, use and give to others).

R(S)HE Learning Objectives: Learn the facts about legal and illegal harmful substances and associated risks, including smoking, alcohol use and drug taking.

Resources:
Diagram of human body to label and word bank.
Use of iPads/secondary sources:

- Effects of energy drinks. https://www.dailymail.co.uk/health/article-3276149/How-energy-drinks-perk-causing-jitters-increased-sweating-new-graphics-reveal-real-affects-body.html
- Office for National Statistics. https://www.ons.gov.uk/
- Online quiz reinforcing ideas about medicines, legal and illegal drugs (limited number of 'free' goes). http://www.educationquizzes.com/ks2/personal-social-and-health-education/drugs/

Key Vocabulary: Human, body, impact, evidence, smoking, drugs, legal, illegal, alcohol, heart, stomach, liver, kidneys, lungs, air sacs (alveoli), brain, mouth, fingers, toes, blood vessels.

Health and Safety: be sensitive to the fact that students may have witnessed drug/alcohol abuse within the family.

Introduction: Ask questions to explore what your pupils know about drugs: What are drugs? Are all drugs bad? How do you know? Display key vocabulary and allow time for discussion and feedback.

Investigation:
What is the impact of legal and illegal substances on the population of the UK? Share a set of pictures of the following: cigarettes/ smoking, alcohol, drugs (including medicines) and energy drinks.

Inform pupils that they will be researching information about a legal or illegal substance to create and deliver an oral presentation to the class, which specifically answers the investigation question.

Activity 1:
How do energy drinks affect the human body? Provide children with an information sheet (see suggested website) and a blank template of a human body with organs. Ask pupils to identify and annotate the parts of the body that are affected by energy drinks, with the effects. What conclusions can be drawn from the evidence? You could use this as an opportunity to update children on any changes to legislation on energy drinks and sugar tax.

Activity 2:
In small mixed-ability groups, provide a large sheet of paper with a picture of *one* of the substances in the middle. They will prepare a presentation about this substance only. Allow 10 minutes for them to write at least three of their own questions which might help them answer the investigation. Circulate to check for appropriate questions and prompt where necessary.

Together, develop a set of criteria that should be included in their presentations, to ensure they have answered the investigation by the end, e.g.:

- Examples of substances, e.g. cocaine, heroin, etc.
- What the substances are made of and how they are made.
- Parts of the body affected by the substance – label a diagram of human body and add brief description of how it is affected, as per the model used in Activity 1.
- Impact of this substance on the diet if appropriate, e.g. alcohol = weight gain.

- Current national health statistics linked to this substance, e.g. more than 120,000 people die each year in the UK from diseases caused by smoking. This could be compared with global statistics, e.g. 7,000,000 deaths per year, and changes over time.

In their groups, invite the pupils to use secondary sources and the suggested websites to conduct research and prepare their poster and oral presentation poster.

Consolidation – during each groups' presentation, all students watching must complete a brief evaluation sheet on each other's presentations to show: what went well; three key facts learned; and any questions they have. Final presentations could be displayed in the classroom to provide an holistic picture of the impacts of drugs, alcohol and smoking on the body.

Plenary: 'Play' the PSHE Drugs quiz (see website link listed above) as a whole class and discuss the answers.

Future/Next Lesson: Recap on presentations delivered. How would you use this knowledge to inform the public of your findings? Write a persuasive letter to a local MP/councillor outlining your evidence, adding any suggestions you might have to support the use of, or reduce the use of, that substance in the community.

Reflection

This investigation is an excellent opportunity to engage with secondary sources!

Could pupils find out the statistics for their local community (using the Office for National Statistics webpage) and compare with neighbouring boroughs? Can they identify any trends or patterns? If so, what could the reasons be for this?

Aside from the impacts on the human body, what impacts of these substances are there on the environment/families/local communities?

Points to consider and conclusion

The process of working scientifically, as included in these PSHE/R(S)HE lessons, enables children to explore the world around them through making careful observations, to question the given and empowers them to seek solutions. They include opportunities to perform simple tests, observe closely, identify and classify and gather and record data to help in answering questions. Ideally primary science should not be compartmentalized, and this combined approach enables educators to build 'science capital' and confidence, as well as key skills for healthy life.

Points to consider for your own setting

- Some pupils may, unfortunately, be familiar with legal and illegal substance abuse through experiences at home. It is important to be sensitive to your cohort and aware that these pupils may be experiencing parenting deficits, maltreatment and less secure attachment patterns.
- Different cultures engage in different handwashing practices. It would be useful to explore the different handwashing techniques that are being engaged with in your school community.
- How does your setting support good handwashing practices?

Key reading

- Pan London Assessment Network (PLAN) (2020) *Working Scientifically Y1-2 Matrix*. Available online: https://www.ase.org.uk/resources/working-scientifically-y1-2-matrix (accessed 19 May 2020).
- Pan London Assessment Network (PLAN) (2020) *Working Scientifically Y5-6 Matrix*. Available online: https://www.ase.org.uk/resources/working-scientifically-y5-6-matrix (accessed 19 May 2020).

Further reading

- The Association of UK Dieticians (2018) *Energy drinks and young people.* Available online: https://www.bda.uk.com/resource/energy-drinks-and-young-people.html (accessed 19 May 2020).

- The Christopher Winter Project (2020) *Teaching Drug and Alcohol Education with Confidence in Primary Schools,* London: PSHE Association.
- Kings College London Enterprising Science and STEM Learning (2016) *Science capital made clear.* Available online: https://www.stem.org.uk/sites/default/files/pages/downloads/Science-Capital-Made-Clear.pdf (accessed 19 May 2020).
- Microbiology Society (2012) *The Why, When and How of Hand Washing.* Available online: https://www.ase.org.uk/resources/why-when-and-how-hand-washing (accessed 19 May 2020).

References

Archer, L. (2015), *Science Capital – an introduction.* Available online: https://www.sciencecentres.org.uk/resources/science-capital/science-capital-introduction/ (accessed 1 October 2019).

Department for Education (DfE) (2013), *Science programmes of study: key stages 1 and 2 National Curriculum in England.* Available online: https://assets.publishing.service.gov.uk/government/uploads/system/uploads/attachment_data/file/425618/PRIMARY_national_curriculum_-_Science.pdf (accessed 14 August 2019).

Department for Education (DfE) (2019a), *Pupil absence in schools in England: 2017 – 2018.* Available online: https://assets.publishing.service.gov.uk/government/uploads/system/uploads/attachment_data/file/787463/Absence_3term_201718_Text.pdf (accessed 1 September 2019).

Department for Education (DfE) (2019b), *Relationships Education, Relationships and Sex Education (RSE) and Health Education.* Available online: https://assets.publishing.service.gov.uk/government/uploads/system/uploads/attachment_data/file/805781/Relationships_Education__Relationships_and_Sex_Education__RSE__and_Health_Education.pdf (accessed 13 August 2019).

Hoath, L. (2019), 'Why science matters: WHAT IS AT THE CORE?', *Primary Science,* 157: 8–9.

Langley, M. (2018), *Science Capital: making science relevant.* Available online: https://www.stem.org.uk/news-and-views/opinions/science-capital-making-science-relevant (accessed 12 May 2020).

National Health Service (NHS) (2016), *How to wash your hands.* Available online: https://www.nhs.uk/live-well/healthy-body/best-way-to-wash-your-hands/ (accessed 1 September 2019).

Ofsted (2019), *Intention and substance: further findings on primary school science from phase 3 of Ofsted's curriculum research.* Available online: https://www.gov.uk/government/publications/intention-and-substance-primary-school-science-curriculum-research (accessed 13 August 2019).

PSHE Association (2017), *A curriculum for life: The case for statutory Personal, Social, Health and Economic (PSHE) Education.* Available online : https://www.pshe-association.org.uk/system/files/Curriculum%20for%20life%20December%20 2017%2012.06%2019%20Dec.pdf (accessed 15 August 2019).

PSHE Association (2020), *Programme of Study for PSHE Education.* Available online: https://www.pshe-association.org.uk/curriculum-and-resources/resources/ programme-study-pshe-education-key-stages-1%E2%80%935 (accessed 12 May 2020).

Turner, C. (2016), 'School exclusions for drugs and alcohol at ten-year high as "county lines" gangs are blamed', *The Telegraph,* 30 April. Available online: https://www. telegraph.co.uk/education/2019/04/30/school-exclusions-drugs-alcohol-ten-year- high-county-lines-gangs/ (accessed 1 August 2019).

7

There's More to RE

Karen Bubb

This chapter explores:

- How RE, alongside PSHE and R(S)HE, can offer engaging and purposeful learning that can prepare children for life's experiences;
- How the use of off-site religious visits can be beneficial to PSHE and R(S)HE;
- That RE is not all about religion!

Whilst discussing Religious Education (RE) with a group of teachers, they recalled and shared their experiences of RE whilst they were in primary school. The memories of RE included: colouring; completing worksheets; learning bible stories; re-writing religious stories; visiting churches and the Christmas nativity to name a few. The general feeling amongst the group was of RE being an instructional subject, unmotivating and somewhat distanced from their lives, some even questioned its place within the primary curriculum. There were however some teachers who gave examples of a subject which interested and intrigued them to learn about different religions and cultures with some sharing recent positive experiences of RE whilst in school. During my career as a primary teacher and more recently as a lecturer of Primary RE on an Initial Teacher Education course (ITT), it has been observed that both trainees' and teachers' feelings towards teaching RE in the primary classroom can often be distorted by their own, sometimes negative, experiences of RE in school. Whilst within RE there is a place for learning bible stories and other activities described by the teachers, it can be, and in my opinion should be, about so much more.

Recently, it has been recognized that RE in primary schools has 'significantly changed its approach in response to the changing nature of society' (Commission on Religious Education, 2018) and is continuing to make improvements with research conducted by the Commission on Religious Education (CoRE) commending the excellent practice taking place in some primary schools (2018). Concurring, an All-Party Parliamentary Group (APPG) report recognized an 'overall improvement in the provision for and the quality of RE' (2013). Since the introduction of the new National Curriculum in 2014, RE remains a statutory subject, maintaining to promote children's spiritual, moral and cultural development (Department for Education, 2014). In addition, schools are also expected to uphold and promote 'Fundamental British Values', often this expectation falls towards the blurred lines of RE, R(S)HE and PSHE under the name of Spiritual, Moral, Social and Cultural (SMSC) development. Whilst there are lots of similarities and connections between RE, PSHE and R(S)HE, this chapter does not advocate that these subjects should be taught in a cross-curricular manner: these subjects have an important place in their own right within the primary curriculum and when taught well these subjects can complement each other (DfE, 2019; Miller, 2014). Experiences shared by trainee teachers, current teachers and personal experiences from visiting schools, highlight the vulnerability of RE, PSHE and R(S)HE within the busy primary classroom, consequently it is pertinent to find methods of teaching these vital subjects alongside each other (Conroy et al, 2014).

The teaching of RE, PSHE and R(S)HE can be very rewarding, knowing that the information and experiences provided for the pupils will aid their ability to live healthily, safely, having a knowledge and understanding about the difference between people and be able to live respectfully alongside one another. But the teaching of these subjects does not come without its issues, some might say more so than other subjects in the National Curriculum. When planning, teaching and assessing these more vulnerable subjects, the teacher must consider how, when teaching, they will be inclusive to all of society and avoid discriminating against the protected characteristics of: age, disability, gender reassignment, marriage and civil partnership, pregnancy and maternity, race, religion or belief, sex and sexual orientation (Equality Act, 2010). Whilst schools are expected to uphold the requirements of the Equality Act 2010 at all times, it is during these lessons that the protected characteristics may be the focus of sometimes difficult and sensitive discussions. In recent DfE guidance on R(S)HE, religion and RE are specifically mentioned with the requirement for schools to demonstrate a 'good understanding of pupils' faith backgrounds and positive relationships between the school and local faith communities help to create a constructive context for the teaching of these subjects', (DfE, 2019: 12). Further connections between these subjects can be seen when teaching R(S)HE, where a thorough knowledge and understanding of religious beliefs and practices of pupils in school, and those of local religious groups, can ensure that topics can be discussed in an inclusive and sensitive manner. When discussing issues such as marriage, violence against girls and women, sexuality, Female Genital Mutilation (FGM) and other religious/non-religious practices relating to sex and relationships, it is vital that the teacher has a knowledge of how the different groups consider these sensitive issues in order not to offend, disrespect or discriminate against any personal beliefs. These lessons should connect a community through a mutual understanding, but if not treated carefully and sensitively they can cause the exact opposite. Whilst the teacher is required to consider the inclusivity of their teaching, they are in a unique position amongst the pupils and the community as they are role models, promoting positive, respectful relationships which should in theory help promote community cohesion.

The sensitive nature of these subjects may attribute to the nervousness displayed by many primary trainee teachers and current teachers, those that I have taught and those within the findings of the CoRE report on RE which concludes many teachers lack confidence in teaching RE (CoRE, 2018: 46). The CoRE report succeeds that of Ofsted (2010) who contributed the lack of training during Initial Teacher Education (ITE) courses and the lack of subject knowledge and understanding of people's beliefs to the poor and sometimes non-existent teaching of RE. In addition to this, teachers may have concerns that the sensitive nature of these subjects may cause tensions with parents, especially as they should consider the rights of parents to withdraw their children from the teaching of RE and R(S)HE (DfE, 2019; National Curriculum Framework for RE, 2013). If parents do act upon this right it is worth speaking with them, inviting them in to look at resources and being available for them to address any concerns they may have. Personal experience has shown that often a lack of understanding of the content of these lessons can cause anxiety and worry for parents and many, once they are aware of the content and the sensitive approach taken to these lessons, often allow their children to participate. This is further recognized in the R(S)HE guidance, stating, 'Good communication and opportunities for parents to understand and ask questions about the school's approach help increase confidence in the curriculum', (DfE, 2019: 17).

So far the links between RE, R(S)HE and PSHE have been highlighted and the remainder of this chapter will demonstrate how the creative potential of these subjects can increase the possible links and adaptability to each other (James and Stern, 2019) through the use of case studies and ideas for planning, teaching and assessing and utilizing out-of-classroom visits.

Examples from practice (KS1) – A walk around the local area

A walk to the local parish church or the nearest Jewish synagogue would seem to have a predominantly RE focus, indeed such as visit would improve the pupils' subject knowledge, help learn the names of objects and people, but it is where places and artefacts become real things and not just a picture in a book. Additionally, these types of visits provide opportunities for building pupils' experiences of traditions, diversity, community, family life, relationships, etc., linking to the PSHE and R(S)HE core themes and aims (PSHE Association, 2017; DfE, 2019).

When partaking in out-of-the-classroom visits there is the tendency to ply the children with worksheets on clipboards to keep them busy. Whilst there may be a time and place for this type of activity they often overshadow the opportunities for children to observe, think and reflect on the environment they are in. It is during these 'down times' that children are more likely to experience those awe and wonder moments. This was observed whilst taking a group of Year 1 pupils to a local cathedral. Much to the confusion of the visiting public, the pupils were asked to lie down on the cathedral floor, gasps of 'wow', 'look at that' and 'isn't the floor cold', soon started to be heard as the children lay there looking at the vast, decorative ceiling above them. Not only did this experience delight the children's vision but it also prompted their curiosity and they were bursting with questions. Learning away from the constraints of the classroom indeed can promote a questioning pedagogy as children are stimulated from the environment they are immersed in: this should be harnessed, not brushed over because the visit must progress onto the next part. When planning visits outside of the classroom, it is important to consider when and how best to facilitate opportunities for children to have some 'down time' and opportunities for them to ask questions. As we know, it is good practice for the teacher to carry out a pre-visit reconnaissance, perhaps during this visit the teacher could find suitable places for such 'down time' to occur. The teacher will also need to consider how and when the pupils' questions can be answered, either during the visit or once back in the classroom. Could the teacher, the TA or a parent helper record their questions which could be answered once back in school? Could the children be videoed at the scene asking their questions? By giving children opportunities to ask questions also acts as an indicator of the children's current knowledge and interests: this information can be used to plan further learning opportunities and crucially identify any misconceptions the children may have.

Reflection

- Chat to the EYFS team in your school, how do they incorporate outdoor learning?
- Are there ways your school can make the local community more accessible?

It is common and good practice for children in EYFS (Early Years Foundation Stage) and KS1 (Key Stage 1) to spend time learning outside of the classroom, making 'learning relevant to real-life contexts' (James and Stern, 2019). The LOTC (Learning Outside the Classroom) organization advocates the valuable learning that can take place outside of the classroom, particularly for early years children. The links to RE and PSHE with this type of learning are intangible, as seen in the KS1 example. Activities such as those described in the visit to the local community and church adhere to the Department for Children, School and Families (2010: 7) guidance, suggesting these opportunities 'contribute to pupils' personal development and wellbeing and to community cohesion by promoting mutual respect and tolerance in a diverse society' and is in conjunction with the core themes of the PSHE Association's programme of study for PSHE of Health and Wellbeing, Relationships and Living in the Wider World (PSHE Association, 2017).

Parents' have the initial role of introducing their children to their family and community and the relationships within them (DfE, 2019). Upon starting school these relationships broaden as children develop friendships with peers and develop relationships with teachers and adults employed in school. For RE, PSHE and R(S)HE the local area offers opportunities for learning to become real life and purposeful, putting learning into a context familiar to the children. For instance, a walk to the local high street can offer opportunities for learning about communities, employment, economics, family relationships, religious traditions, local history and importantly it should arouse pupils' curiosity. The new R(S)HE guidance outlines what pupils should know by the end of primary school and several aims specifically link to opportunities of such visits described in this case study. The aims include:

> that others' families, either in school or in the wider world, sometimes look different from their family, but that they should respect those differences and know that other children's families are also characterized by love and care.
>
> DfE, 2019: 20

> the importance of respecting others, even when they are very different from them (for example, physically, in character, personality or backgrounds), or make different choices or have different preferences or beliefs'.
>
> DfE, 2019: 21

> that in school and in wider society they can expect to be treated with respect by others, and that in turn they should show due respect to others, including those in positions of authority.
>
> DfE, 2019: 21

Examples from practice (KS2) – Developing community cohesion

As with the KS1 case study, learning opportunities outside of the classroom can be a valuable experience for several reasons. Places of worship, when visited correctly, can enhance the teaching and learning of RE (McCreery, Palmer and Voiels, 2008) by bringing the religion to life, allowing children to experience the religion with all of their senses. However, visits can offer so much more, especially in terms of the PSHE and R(S)HE for the children. The example below discusses a visit with a group of Year 5 (predominantly white, middle-class children) who attend a rural village school (with no religious affiliation).

During a visit to a local mosque we were greeted by the Iman wearing his transitional muslin clothing, with a full beard, hat, etc. immediately supporting the stereotype of 'a Muslim' that many children (and adults) have. On entering the mosque, we took off our shoes and the females amongst us donned our headscarves amidst the giggles from some of the children. The children were given a guided tour with the key features of the mosque being pointed out; the children sketched them in almost silence. Even the most adventurous and outgoing children in the class seemed to be in awe of what they were being shown and hardly spoke a word. After being generously invited to partake in squash and cakes, the children were invited to ask the Iman questions, it seemed the sugar had filled them with a little more confidence and soon they were chatting away to the Iman and other helpers at the mosque. Interestingly many of the questions did not relate particularly to what they had been shown in the mosque but more about the lifestyle of a believer of Islam. For example, one child asked, 'How do you pray when you don't know which way is East?', to which the Iman replied casually, 'I have an app on my phone!'. Without a blink of an eye the children moved on to the next question, whilst I sat there in awe of the children's acceptance of his answer. 'Do you like wearing those clothes?' asked another: the Iman himself smirked at this question and replied rhetorically with 'Do you think I wear these all of the time?', going on to explain he usually wears jeans and a jumper but he thought he should wear the traditional clothes to show the children. The children nodded in acknowledgement of his efforts to look good for them and continued with their questions. Questions flowed and both the Iman and the children seemed to be enjoying the informal, friendly chat that was taking place. Even the more sensitive questions about women wearing the Niqab or Burqa were answered honestly and openly – you could almost feel the mutual respect between the Iman and the pupils. Particularly refreshing was though the children innocently asked what many might have deemed as sensitive questions, the Iman answered these in such a matter of fact way that no issues were even considered.

Reflection

- When planning a trip to a place of worship, consider the other areas of the curriculum that could also benefit from the visit.

Whilst on the surface, the visit to the mosque focused on learning about Islam and indeed it did, on returning to school my thoughts were cast to how much more could be learnt apart from the obvious RE. When looking at the aims from the National Curriculum Framework for Religious Education (NCFRE) the visit covered: 'identify, investigate and respond to questions posed, and responses offered by some of the sources of wisdom found in religions and worldviews' and 'find out about and investigate key concepts and questions of belonging, meaning, purpose and truth, responding creatively', (NCFRE, 2013: 11). It reinforced some of the key subject knowledge that had been learnt in the classroom prior to the visit; it had indeed allowed the children to experience the religion in greater depth. But what did this visit offer in terms of PSHE and R(S)HE? Instead of writing a recount of the visit (a typically mundane task set following a visit), the children were asked to talk with their peers about what had been the most memorable part of the visit. Apart from the squash and cake, many of the children spoke of the question time with the Iman and other volunteers at the mosque, they seemed to be more interested in how people following Islam live rather than the aspects of the mosque they were shown. It dawned on me at that point that the children had learnt far more than the features of a mosque, the visit had served a much wider important purpose. In a subconscious way it had boosted positive relationships with local communities, these children with little experience of seeing, let alone meeting anyone from the Islamic faith would be able to go out into the wider world with a better understanding of what it means to follow Islam. The visit had asked them to consider their own stereotypes. The CoRE report suggests that places of worship visits 'will enable young people to develop their understanding of the ways in which different people interpret and engage with institutional worldviews' (CoRE, 2018: 76) and in connection with this the PSHE programme of study states a core theme of 'Living in the Wider world' throughout all of the key stages (PSHE Association, 2017).

Point to consider for your own setting

It is hoped with the improvements currently being seen in primary schools, that RE, PSHE and R(S)HE will cement their place as individual subjects in the primary curriculum. In order to support these improvements, teachers and those training to be the teachers of the future need up-to-date and research-informed training. With research suggesting that many teachers lack confidence and regard their training as non-existent or very limited, many are particularly concerned about their own subject knowledge and have the fear of saying something wrong and upsetting people regarding their beliefs. As a teacher educator, my role in this is crucial, to instil the passion for these vulnerable subjects in the future primary teachers so that on entering their career they too see the importance of these subjects and will ensure they are included in their timetables.

For those already in teaching, Continued Professional Development (CPD) is vital to provide not only subject knowledge, but more importantly giving teachers the confidence to plan, teach and assess these special subjects. This chapter has demonstrated how R(S)HE and PSHE are already intertwined within RE, the links are there and schools now need to make those links an obvious part in their school curriculum.

Key reading

- Commission on Religious Education (CoRE) (2018), *Final report: Religion and worldviews: the way forward a national plan for RE.* Available from: https://www.commissiononre.org.uk/wp-content/uploads/2018/09/Final-Report-of-the-Commission-on-RE.pdf

Further reading

- Grigg, R. and Russell, S. V. (2018), *Teaching primary humanities,* Oxon: Routledge.
- Webster, M. (2010), *Creative approaches to teaching Primary RE,* London: Routledge.

References

All-Party Parliament Group (2013), *RE: The Truth Unmasked.* Available online: http://religiouseducationcouncil.org.uk (accessed 4 September 2019).

Commission on Religious Education (CoRE) (2018), *Final report: Religion and worldviews: the way forward a national plan for RE.* Available online: https://www.commissiononre.org.uk/wp-content/uploads/2018/09/Final-Report-of-the-Commission-on-RE.pdf (accessed 10 September 2019).

Conroy, J., Lundie, R., Davis, V., Baumfield, P., Barnes, T., Gallagher, K., Lowden, N., Borque and Wenell, K. (2014), *Does religious education work? A multi-dimensional investigation,* London: Bloomsbury.

Department for Children, School and Families (2010), *Religious Education English Schools: Non-statutory guidance,* Nottingham: DCSF.

Department for Education (DfE) (2014), *The National Curriculum for England; framework for key stages 1-4.* Available online: https://www.gov.uk/government/publications/national-curriculum-in-england-framework-for-key-stages-1-to-4/the-national-curriculum-in-england-framework-for-key-stages-1-to-4 (accessed 18 September 2019).

Department for Education (DfE) (2019), *Relationships Education, Relationships and Sex Education (RSE) and Health Education.* Available online: https://www.gov.uk/government/publications/relationships-education-relationships-and-sex-education-rse-and-health-education (accessed 10 September 2019).

James, M. and Stern, J. (2019), *Mastering Primary Religious Education.* London: Bloomsbury.

Learning Outside the Classroom (no date), *Council for Learning Outside the Classroom.* Available online: https://www.lotc.org.uk/ (accessed 12 September 2019).

McCreery, E., Palmer, S. and Voiels, V. (2008), *Teaching Religious Education,* Exeter: Learning Matters.

Miller, J. (2014), *Religion, education, community and relations: some reflections on the APPG inquiry.* Available online: https://www.religiouseducationcouncil.org.uk/wp-content/uploads/2017/10/Religion_education_community_relati.pdf (accessed 11 August 2019).

National Curriculum Framework for Religious Education (NCFRE) (2013). Available online: http://resubjectreview.recouncil.org.uk/media/file/RE_Review_Summary.pdf (accessed 19 September 2019).

Ofsted (2010), *Transforming Religious Education.* Available online: www.medway.gov.uk/pdf/OFSTED%20Transforming%20RE%20June%202010_2.pdf (accessed 8 November 2019).

Parliament. House of Lords (2010), *Equality Act 2010.* Available online: http://www.legislation.gov.uk/ukpga/2010/15 (accessed 10 September 2019).

PSHE Association (2017), *Programmes of study.* Available online: https://www.pshe-association.org.uk/curriculum-and-resources/resources/programme-study-pshe-education-key-stages-1%E2%80%935 (accessed 11 September 2019).

8

Tackling PSHE and R(S)HE through PE

Daniel Hughes

This chapter explores:

- How PE can be a vehicle to support the teaching of PSHE and R(S)HE;

- The impact of PE on children's wellbeing and health in relation to PSHE and R(S)HE;

- An inclusive PE curriculum that encourages collaborative learning.

Physical education has the power to transform children's lives. It has multiple benefits: it can help to promote a healthy lifestyle; develop a child's self-esteem; encourage a strong sense of responsibility; and forge a deep-rooted sense of community. When children enjoy and relish physical education, and the joys that come with it, their personal development and educational progress are positively affected. Physical education not only helps develop the body physically through physical activity; it also supports cognition, mental health and how a person can be decisive with their life choices. It helps young people acquire the knowledge, understanding and skills they need to manage their lives now and in the future (PSHE Association, 2017).

This chapter will look at how personal, social and health education can be developed by focusing on physical education, as well as noting the benefits in relationship education that can come from collaboration and team activities. It aims to demonstrate how, by encouraging children to take an active role in their physical development and developing an inclusive, well-rounded physical education curriculum, it can work alongside the PSHE and R(S)HE curricula to create more responsible and self-aware children. It will argue that PE can help build a sense of identity within all children and support the creation of communities within schools.

PSHE and R(S)HE working together with PE

The National Curriculum's aims for PE include leading 'healthy, active lives' and achieving 'their personal best' (DfE, 2013). The United Nations Educational, Scientific and Cultural Organisation (UNESCO) (2015) claimed in their Quality physical education guidelines that physical education makes children healthier, and the joys of sport and physical exercise are essential to all. With a growing crisis around obesity and sedentary lifestyles, the impact of physical activity cannot be understated. In recent times, there was the commitment to two hours of high-quality PE (Ofsted, 2013), with a push to reach three hours through PE and out of hours sport (DfE, 2013). Within primary schools, the majority of this time will be in PE lessons, but with the aforementioned time-restricted curriculum, playtimes and after-school clubs provide additional opportunities to develop this. Following the 2012 London Olympics, this renewed focus has been supported by PE and sport premium funding that has to be justifiably spent by primary schools to promote sport and physical activity. High-stakes testing and accountability measures are arguably squeezing the curriculum, therefore finding the time and space for physical exercise is becoming more challenging year on year. With a focus on PSHE and R(S)HE leading the PE curriculum, as well as using PE as a vehicle to tackle the statutory R(S)HE curriculum, it can be argued that PSHE and R(S)HE can be strengthened and developed through physical activity.

The links between PSHE and R(S)HE and the PE curriculum are numerous. Within the statutory R(S)HE and health statutory guidance (DfE, 2019), there is a clear focus on physical health and wellbeing. Some links can also be made with relationships education, which emphasizes positive relationships, the deliberate cultivation of character traits and positive personal attributes (DfE, 2019). By identifying the clear links, the government have acknowledged the importance of ensuring all children take part in physical activity, noting that it impacts on both their physical health and mental health. By focusing on physical activity within PSHE and R(S)HE lessons, using it as a vehicle to aid children's personal development, the benefits of physical activity are numerous. Consider each of the aspects below and how these can be supported in PE and the classroom:

- Mental health can be enhanced with links between physical activity and mental health made explicit.
- Wellbeing and self-esteem can be promoted.
- Improving the understanding and development of relationships and collaboration with others.
- Manage emotions and develop self-care techniques.

- Understanding when and how to seek support from others.
- Establishing and building routines through regular exercise.
- Developing personal goals and understanding how to achieve these.

As subjects that naturally complement each other, PE and PSHE and R(S)HE can work together to develop children holistically. The R(S)HE and Health curriculum states explicitly that 'emphasis should be given to the positive two-way relationship between good physical health and mental well-being' (DfE, 2019: 32). Moving forward, we will now look at how this can be created, considering theoretical perspectives and case studies to see the benefits of combining both elements.

Creating an inclusive environment

Creating an environment and a climate that allows children to explore, investigate and lead their learning is an essential aspect of physical education. Child-led approaches remove the need for heavy teacher instruction and allow children to exercise and enjoy their physical activity. Too often, a prevailing sense of control, possibly borne out of strict health and safety measures, prevents children from exploring all of the opportunities a game, dance or gymnastic activity has to offer. A motivational climate, as explored by Morgan (2017), allows for this and places children's personal and social education at the heart of lessons. To enable this, children need to take responsibility for their learning and make decisions that can improve their understanding. Teachers can take on the role of facilitator, creating opportunities for children to design their activities. A motivational climate is created by considering psychological, sociological and pedagogical aspects of lessons and environments. Incorporating a practical framework, with a mastery climate as the prevalent focus opposed to a competitive ego-driven climate, is critical. The mastery climate gives children leadership roles and gets them involved in decision-making, self-referenced goals and the private recognition of achievements. This then improves children's intrinsic motivational development. An ego climate, in contrast, is teacher-led, includes public recognition of achievements and use of ability groups. Therefore, to create personal, health and social educational opportunities, a motivational climate of inclusion, that places the child at the centre of their learning is fundamental as opposed to an ego-driven one. This will create the right atmosphere within PE-based sessions, where all children can achieve their personal goals.

Think about ...

Working with the class early in the year to develop the culture within both PSHE and R(S)HE and PE lessons. Look to co-construct rules and behaviours expected with the children and look at scenarios together, discussing the best approach to take to maintain high levels of motivation.

Personal development

Physical activity can support personal development. Including children in setting and planning their goals in lessons and over a more extended period of time is critical. This can range from trying to win a game, run a quicker time or perform a dance at a higher standard. Children, by their very nature, will compare themselves with others, so creating an atmosphere where mastery goals are the focus rather than performance goals (Senko et al., 2011) is vital. Achievement goal theory (Dweck, 1986, cited in Senko, et al., 2011) advocates that increasing effort will help achieve self-defined criteria and applying this concept in the classroom is challenging. Focused on a mastery approach opposed to attempting to out-perform their peers, this presents difficulties. Children can naturally want to compare themselves to others. Deciding how to involve children in setting their own goals is essential. They can generate success criteria, review their performance through the use of video or peer-to-peer support. Agreeing on guidelines and modelling how to provide feedback can support children who are unsure. Equally, praising children for achieving their personal goals rather than comparing and contrasting performances is a position that the class teacher should take when delivering any form of PE. It is helpful to consider a child who is set unrealistic goals; their chances of success are much smaller than if they have co-constructed their goals. PSHE begins with reference to 'personal' education; setting goals, achieving these and having a sense of personal satisfaction can be reached immediately and over a longer period of time through participation in various physical activities.

> *Think about . . .*
>
> *Outdoor adventure activities are a perfect example of this; a key strand in the PE curriculum, it does not need to be restricted to a residential in Year 6. Problem-solving activities and risk-taking can be treaded throughout an OAA scheme of work that strengthens children's development.*

Relationship building

Physical activity naturally lends itself to building relationships. At the beginning of this chapter, it was suggested that it could create communities and a sense of belonging. Within the new statutory framework, building, maintaining and forming relationships and establishing communities impacts positively on the health and wellbeing of all involved:

> This teaching should make clear that people are social beings and that spending time with others, taking opportunities to consider the needs of others and practising service

to others, including in organised and structured activities and groups are beneficial for health and wellbeing.

DfE, 2019: 32

PE has its foundations in collaboration. There are individual elements and activities, but often it involves being part of a team or supporting teammates and partners to achieve their successes. This usually requires structure and modelling. Teachers need to allow time for this to progress and form. The competitive element within lessons can help or hinder successful relationships building. If winning is the only thing that matters and is deemed to make their learning successful, then it will not work for all children. A small percentage of the class will be motivated by winning. However, if achieving self-constructed goals together and with contributions from all involved is how the learning is seen as successful, this will inherently motivate far more children. Fostering a sense of community remains the main challenge. Some may argue that this is intrinsic; the mix of children, the teaching philosophy and the natural chemistry either lends itself to this or does not. A community is a condition of sharing or of having individual attitudes in common. Shared success, rewarding particular attitudes and fostering an agreed vision is the role of the teacher; modelling and the scaffolding of learning behaviours in PE can go a long way to creating positive relationships between the children in a class.

Think about . . .

How do you feel when you win at a game or the team you support wins? How do you feel when you fail at something or your team loses? Everyone experiences these emotions and teachers need to allow for this to happen but teach children how to lose and how to become more resilient.

The following case studies are examples where PSHE and R(S)HE have been the focus of the lessons, with PE being used as the vehicle to drive the learning of the children.

Case Study 1: Key Stage 1

Claire wanted to develop her Year 2's ability to work together, improve their relationships and social interactions and challenge themselves. She developed a series of PSHE and R(S)HE lessons that used PE as a vehicle to help them explore journeys. Beyond the PSHE and R(S)HE focus, there are multiple cross-curricular links here: story-mapping in English to support children's sequencing of events; drawing maps and plans of routes in geography; developing positional vocabulary; developing a knowledge of the natural world; and identifying patterns within the work linking with maths. However, Claire's primary focus was PSHE and R(S)HE.

The topic of journeys had been developed through their English, yet it lent itself heavily to PSHE and R(S)HE. They read several of the journey books, and Claire established their role.

After reading books in a similar vein to *We're Going on a Bear Hunt* by Michael Rosen, *The Journey* by Francesca Sanna or *The Tunnel* by Anthony Browne, she asked the children to imagine that they were going to go on a journey. The aim was to collect something magical. Sorting the children into pairs, she asked them first to draw the magical object that they would be searching for. The children came up with objects such as magical potions, jewellery, mystical stones and treasure chests. This collaborative task allowed the children to use an original, fictional context to explore their relationships. In addition to the magical elements, Claire also asked them to envisage a magical property linked to friendships. The children came up with empathetic, respectful ideas: the object would allow the finders to only say kind words to others for a period of time; it would send you to a safe place protecting you from any dangers; it would help everyone to become friends; and more. This allowed for an exploration of practical steps you can take to improve and construct relationships with others. A fictional purpose can often be as valuable as a real one if approached with the same rigour and enthusiasm. The one Claire focused on was *We're Going on a Bear Hunt*. The variety of elements, levels and direction lent itself actively to creating sequences of movements.

After establishing their magical object, Claire put together a series of physical tasks that the children would complete in pairs and explore journeys further. Firstly, she began by using dance as a tool. The children completed moving actions alongside musical accompaniment, sequencing and moving through a journey in response to the music. Following this, she then used low apparatus to complete simple gymnastics sequences. The children worked together to construct a sequence featuring a series of balances, rolls and jumps, based on travelling through the mud, the wavy grass and the water. Throughout the process, the children were co-constructing their journeys, working together to establish a route.

After the children had designed and developed sequences through both dance and gymnastics, Claire took them outside for a couple of PE lessons. Chalking their journeys on the playground outside, the children re-enacted the journeys, including sports equipment to negotiate and complete. Throughout, Claire was able to build in reflection time; this involved sharing journeys between groups, discussing their ideas and sharing what it was like to work together. The dramatic elements of this physical activity were at the forefront and allowed children to explore their relationships. Further to this, Claire was able to also discuss personal safety, the positive impact of physical activity on their health, and the impact of their magical object. Within all of these role-play scenarios and physical activities, they enacted the finding of the magical object and its resultant powers. Claire noted that the children's relationships developed in the classroom as a result, and she was able to use the co-constructed journeys as a model that could then be applied in other lessons, both metaphorically and literally. Claire was able to make this pertinent observation after completing the PSHE and R(S)HE unit of work:

> *By enacting the journeys physically, using their bodies to explore emotions, cognition and relationship building, the children improved their sense of self. I felt like they were empowered. By including the physical elements to experience the physical and emotional toll that such a journey might involve, they improved their understanding of both themselves and others.*

Links to Relationships Education, Relationships and Sex Education (R(S)HE) and Health Education Statutory Guidance (2019)

Physical health and fitness

By the end of primary school:
Pupils should know:

- The characteristics and mental and physical benefits of an active lifestyle.
- The importance of building regular exercise into daily and weekly routines and how to achieve this.

Links to the PSHE Association's PSHE Education Programme of Study:

PSHE Association Core Theme 2: Relationships Key Stage 1

R5. To listen to other people and play and work co-operatively.
R7. To offer constructive support and feedback to others.

Reflection

Reflecting on the issues within Case Study 1:

- How did the incorporation of games-based pedagogy impact positively on the children and the personal and social development?
- Consider the percentage of time spent with the children working together to development their skills and tactical awareness.
- The impact of more time spent on physical activity on their health and wellbeing, especially in the lessons following this session.

This example was founded on an environment that was supportive and encouraged while giving the children ownership of their learning. Collaboration is essential when approaching games, with elements of sportsmanship. The following example illustrates the challenges that teachers face:

I understand that PE is vital. But it's skills and drills; that way, I can manage the class effectively and ensure everyone stays safe.

Case Study 2: Key Stage 2

Susan wanted to develop her Year 6 class' interactions and ability to collaborate. In agreement with Year 1 colleagues, she established a sports leaders training programme. Based over six sessions, it involved giving her class the responsibility of designing, managing and administrating physical activities and games with the younger children in the school.

To begin with, Susan asked the children to agree on the qualities of leadership and how these might look in action. From this task, many benefits arose. It gave the children the chance to decide on what respectful, meaningful relationships might involve and how they were going to be role models for the younger children. Understanding who they were working with and their responsibilities was a significant starting point. Alongside this, they considered the skills, attributes and qualities needed, reflecting on their personal development. There was also some scenario work; if a younger child misbehaved, how would they respond? If there was falling out, how can this be resolved? The children decided that communication, respect and patience were required.

Afterwards, the children set about creating several lessons, learning small-sided games and activities they could carry out with the Key Stage 1 pupils. These were linked to the National Curriculum, introducing a competitive task or skill that would develop children's balance, coordination or agility. Many of these games were taught to the Year 6 children; then time was spent developed their games to use. These allowed them to collaborate and increase the levels of ownership over the delivery. Each group created a task card – a document of their activity and how it can be used with the younger children. Time was given to facilitate the activities, and the Year 6 children began to run these during lunchtimes.

Links to Relationships Education, Relationships and Sex Education (R(S)HE) and Health Education Statutory Guidance (2019)

Respectful relationships

By the end of primary school:
Pupils should know:

- The importance of respecting others
- Practical steps they can take in a range of different contexts to improve or support respectful relationships.

Links to the PSHE Association's PSHE Education Programme of Study:

PSHE Association Core Theme 2: Relationships Key Stage 2

R1. To recognise and respond appropriately to a wider range of feelings in others
R11. To work collaboratively towards shared goals

Reflection

Sports leadership can be an influential and instructive process for all children.

Reflecting on the issues within this case-study, consider the following points:

- What would the next steps for these children be?
- Could this be adapted for different ages or is it exclusively for upper key stage 2?
- How can you encourage independence and leadership within smaller lessons and in those without any form of physical activity?

Points to consider and conclusion

This chapter has explored how PE can be delivered with a focus on personal, social and health education. Personal and social education must be the central focus of the PE curriculum, rather than a skills-centric, drills and teacher-instructional focus dominating pedagogical discourses. The case studies and ideas within this chapter emphasize not only the obvious health benefits of PE but how relationship development can explicitly be at the heart of lessons where PE is being used as the primary vehicle. It helps support intra-personal and inter-personal development and builds self-esteem and wellbeing. When planning PSHE and R(S)HE lessons, using PE can create a community spirit within children; this, in turn, helps develop children's sense of identity.

Points to consider for your own setting

- What is the culture and atmosphere within PE lessons?
- How do staff view PE? What experiences did they have of PE when they were younger and how does this affect their delivery of PE?
- Within PE lessons, is the primary focus on skills or can it be adapted to personal attributes and motivations?

 # Key reading

- Griggs, G. (2015), *Understanding Primary Physical Education*, London: Routledge.

Further reading

- Dyson, B. and Casey, A. (eds) (2012), *Cooperative Learning in Physical Education*, London: Routledge.
- Howells, K., Carney, A., Castle, N. and Little, R. (2018), *Mastering Primary Physical Education*, London: Bloomsbury.

References

- Department for Education (DfE) (2013), *National Curriculum.* Available online: https://www.gov.uk/government/collections/national-curriculum (accessed 18 November 2019).
- Department for Education (DfE) (2019), *Relationships Education, Relationships and Sex Education (RSE) and Health Education.* Available online: https://assets. publishing.service.gov.uk/government/uploads/system/uploads/attachment_data/ file/805781/Relationships_Education__Relationships_and_Sex_Education__R(S) HE__and_Health_Education.pdf (accessed 20 November 2019).
- Ofsted (2013) *Beyond 2012: outstanding physical education for all.* Available at: https://www.gov.uk/government/publications/beyond-2012-outstanding-physical-education-for-all
- PSHE Association (2017), *PSHE Education Programme of Study: Key Stages 1-5.* Available online: https://www.pshe-association.org.uk/curriculum-and-resources/ resources/programme-study-pshe-education-key-stages-1%E2%80%935 (accessed 13 September 2019).
- Morgan, K. (2017), 'Reconceptualizing Motivational Climate in Physical Education and Sport Coaching: An Interdisciplinary Perspective', *Quest,* 69 (1): 95–112.
- Senko, C., Hulleman, C. S. and Harackiewicz (2011), 'Achievement Goal Theory at the Crossroads: Old Controversies, Current Challenges, and New Directions', *Educational Psychologist,* 46 (1): 26–47.

9

'Being' and the Outdoors

Daniel Hughes

This chapter explores:

- How the outdoors can be used in the teaching of PSHE and R(S)HE;
- The benefits of being outside and how it links to the PSHE and R(S) HE curriculum;
- Why the outdoors is a powerful pedagogical tool that can have a significant impact on pupils' personal, social and health development.

Picture the scene. You are stood surrounded by trees staring down at you, and the warm glow of the sun peeking out from between the trunks. The smell of flowers and the buzz of insects fills the air. A bird *caws* in the distance. You can hear the woodland talking to you, the hustle and bustle of life encasing you and giving you a warm feeling inside. You feel alive. This is the power of the outdoors, and how it can affect you physically, emotionally and spiritually. That is the central theme of this chapter; the power of the outdoors.

Being outside is an essential part of education and of being a person. It should be an integral part of each child's education, and PSHE and R(S)HE offers, amongst other subjects, opportunities to use the outdoors to support children's development. Time constraints within the curriculum, anxiety over risk, the weather and the pragmatical approach needed to use the outdoors could be barriers to using it to support learning. A significant amount of research discusses the positive impact of the outdoors, yet this can appear to be very supplemental – how is it supporting their progress with the core subjects? The PSHE and R(S)HE curriculum can be directly supported by the outdoors; this means that the outdoors must be considered a powerful tool that is both under-utilized and overthought. Forest school itself is not enough. Further opportunities must be developed by using the natural environment and positioning the outdoors as a pedagogical approach to tackle PSHE and R(S)HE can help it become a strength. The benefits of outdoors are often linked to performance in the classroom; I would argue that being outdoors is learning for its own sake – any subsequent classroom benefits are a welcome addition.

The outdoors can be an excellent resource to support the PSHE and R(S)HE of children of all ages. Being outside and working in the natural environment can leave a powerful impression on pupils of all ages. Using the outdoors effectively can be challenging, and this chapter will look at how, with careful planning and pupil-led learning, PSHE can be supported through meaningful and purposeful outdoor activities. It will explore how pupils can interact and work in outdoor settings to learn about themselves, each other and the wider world.

The impact and benefits of the outdoors

Young people are spending less time outdoors today than ever before (Council for Learning Outside the Classroom, 2019). Only 8 per cent of children get out of their classrooms into green spaces (Natural England, 2016). There are multiple reasons for this: safety, social media, entertainment, lack of outdoor spaces, housing, crime, parental concerns and other reasons are all equally valid. The critical aspect is that less time is being spent outdoors by young people within England. Although the research is limited, multiple organizations including the Wildlife Trust, the Council for Learning Outside the Classroom and Natural England advocate for the use of the outdoors to be an integral part of a child's education and curriculum. In Scotland, the Curriculum for Excellence through Outdoor Learning places the outdoors as a central pedagogical tool and key motivator of children's educational progress (Learning and Teaching Scotland, 2010). Therefore, if a large amount of relatively new research is suggesting that the outdoors can impact positively on the educational outcomes of young people, using it in connection with the PSHE and R(S)HE curriculum makes them seem natural bedfellows.

In 2016, the National Connections Demonstration project commissioned by Natural England findings were presented and demonstrated how teachers could be empowered to use to help children experience the 'joy of the natural environment' (Natural England, 2016). The findings are significant. It showed that 92 per cent of children were more engaged with learning when outdoors, and 85 per cent of teachers saw a positive impact on behaviour. Interestingly, 79 per cent of teachers felt that it did have a positive effect on their teaching practice. There is clearly some way to go with this and training/professional development needs to be an essential aspect of future work to allow the outdoors to be used successfully with all children and teachers. Christie et al. (2014) noted that this was the main finding from their research into the development of the Curriculum for Excellence through Outdoor Learning.

Juliet Robertson (2014: 2) defines outdoor learning as 'an umbrella term which covers every type of learning experience which happens outdoors. This could be adventurous activities, environmental education, team challenges, an international expedition or a playground game.' She continues by noting that just 'being' outdoors is not enough; experiential learning needs to be facilitated and encouraged. The outdoors has the scope to make a difference, but only if teachers are prepared, trained and knowledgeable about how to use it effectively. Challenges with the outdoors will be explored later in the chapter, but the benefits outweigh the difficulties. Teachers who can embrace the outdoors and use it successfully will notice multiple benefits for all of their children. These benefits are explored further in the next section, and the links with the PSHE and R(S)HE curriculums are identified.

The PSHE and R(S)HE connection to the outdoors

The outdoors has numerous physical benefits. It can improve fitness, physical health and can have an explicit link to mental health and wellbeing. Within the R(S)HE and Health statutory curriculum, the outdoors is specifically mentioned:

> Pupils should know:
>
> The benefits of physical exercise, time outdoors, community participation, voluntary and service-based activity on mental wellbeing and happiness.
>
> DfE, 2019

Therefore, giving them time outdoors begins to address this specific objective. There is also a clear link to children needing to understand about safe and unsafe exposure to the sun, and how self-care is important. If they can understand how being outdoors can improve your wellbeing and directly impact on a person's happiness, this is teaching them vital lessons for them in the future. Marchant et al.'s (2019) research identified the impact that the outdoors can have on children's freedom to express themselves, intrinsic motivation and their emotional health. The outdoors can reduce stress and support cognitive development (Marchant et al., 2019). Having an active lifestyle and how daily exercise are also explicitly mentioned in the R(S)HE and Health curriculum, and the outdoors can undoubtedly be used to address these. Walking to school or cycling are both outdoor activities that are directly noted as possible examples of where this curriculum can be addressed. Incorporating the outdoors will link with the physical health and wellbeing aspects of the curriculum, as long as they are precisely planned for.

The Early Learning Foundation Stage leads the push towards using the outdoors effectively. In previous versions of the Development Matters document, it argued how being outdoors has a positive impact on children's sense of wellbeing and helps all aspects of children's development. An awareness that being outdoors offers opportunities for doing things in different ways and on different scales than when indoors, giving first-hand contact with weather, seasons and the natural world. Outdoor learning environments offer children freedom to explore, use their senses and be physically active and exuberant. Within the EYFS document 'Effective Practice: Outdoor Learning' (DfES, 2007), the key messages are:

1 The outdoor environment has unique characteristics and features.
2 Outdoor learning has equal value to indoor learning.
3 Outdoor learning has a positive impact on children's wellbeing and development.
4 Children need the support of attentive and engaged adults who are enthusiastic about the outdoors and understand the importance of outdoor learning.
5 Outdoor learning is enhanced by an environment that is richly resourced with play materials that can be adapted and used in different ways.
6 An approach to outdoor learning that considers experiences rather than equipment places children at the centre of the provision being made.

These points are pertinent, not only to Early Years but to all primary school-age children. If the emphasis is placed on using the outdoors from an early age and not stopped but developed and continued throughout school, the PSHE and R(S)HE curriculum will automatically be enhanced and promoted through this approach.

Risk-taking and personal development

The outdoors provides opportunities for children's personal development; risk-taking and self-exploration are both key development opportunities and challenges for teachers. By being too protective, teachers and parents can create an overwhelming sense of anxiety and significant challenges for the child's relationship with the outdoors. The outdoors presents a continual changing and fluctuating environment that children need to be able to negotiate and navigate with others and independently. Identifying risks and how they can manage these is critical; Robertson (2014) advocates a positive attitude towards risk, where teachers model and teach how to deal with it when outside. For children's personal development and self-awareness, knowing when and how to tackle risks positively, the outdoors is the best place in which to explore this due to its dynamic and changeable nature. Within the R(S)HE and Health curriculum, being safe is a crucial aspect. Even though it could be argued that it focuses on boundary setting with others and safeguarding issues, going outside presents multiple questions around 'being safe'. Modelling and scenario exploration will have heightened children's safety, both of their own and others. The aims are to tackle risk and improving children's self-management and consequently, their resilience.

The environment and the children's relationship with it

Relationships with others, through friendships and caring, respectful relationships, form a key strand in the R(S)HE and Health curriculum. The outdoors allows for further exploration of a child's relationship with themselves and the wider world. Always prevalent, environmental and climate change are high on the agenda – most young people are aware of the impact of Greta Thunberg and the Extinction Rebellion movements. The PSHE Association curriculum notes that children should have the opportunity to 'research, discuss and debate topical issues' (PSHE Association, 2017: 19). The environment is a significant one. Children should be able to explore their environment and understand the nature within it. With the current focus on climate change and changes to the environment, developing children's understanding of it is crucial for them to make informed decisions about how they will interact with their surroundings as they mature.

Challenges

There is currently a lack of 'outdoor confidence' with teachers (Natural England, 2016). Forest school, a positive development in terms of the outdoors, has had a significant amount of money invested and does not explicitly link to the key concept of *Friluftsliv* – 'the spiritual impact of the outdoors on a person's soul'. However, it is not necessarily being taught correctly in English school – it should be about discovery learning over an extended period, with children involved in meaningful and challenging activities including risk (Lightfoot, 2019). Forest school in England can be a very 'anglified' and watered-down version of the true spirit of Forest school. Lightfoot (2019) argues that this version may not have the benefits initially thought.

Furthermore, it is being used as a marketing tool, but this is not necessarily being fulfilled. Recently, the Wildlife Trust set up 'Nature-Friendly Schools' where teachers will receive training to link learning to the National Curriculum. This is tied closely to the government's 25 Year Environment Plan and has received a £6.4 million sum with the project (Wildlife Trust, 2019). Many of the words relating to the project show that it aims to improve children's wellbeing, mental health and learning, specifically targeted at disadvantaged children. In acknowledging the impact on

PSHE and R(S)HE, and understanding the creation of green, nature-friendly spaces, it could prove significant. The British Educational Research Association (BERA) has also established a Nature Outdoor Learning and Play special interest group to research the impact of the outdoors. A lot of focus is given on empowering teachers to use the outdoors effectively. The following case studies provide examples of how this could be done to support PSHE and R(S)HE lessons in schools.

Case Study 1: Key Stage 1

Originating as a geography topic that she felt was relevant to her children, Sarah decided to investigate the new housing scheme in the local town of her Year 2 children. The local area has several new housing developments happening that were capturing the interest of the children, and this inspired her to develop an outdoor unit of work founded on PSHE and R(S)HE. She was aiming to allow children to opportunity to investigate concepts and ideas, create and construct and imagine the possibilities that the outdoors could offer.

Beginning with an exploration of homes, Sarah collated images of different buildings and children compared and contrasted these. Working together with the constructors, she managed to contact the building organization and arrange a class trip to visit the site and discuss the project with contractors. Companies are often very keen to involve the wider community in their activities; it is often seen as a real positive to work alongside schools. Previously, the school had also been involved in a local council building project where the contractors visited the school to share their plans and talk about the work they were doing. Seizing this opportunity, Sarah was able to take the children there and see the work being done to construct the homes but also consider the impact on the environment.

After completing this, the class began to work in collaborative groups to construct a community. Using building resources used initially for Forest school, the children drew, sketched and considered the homes they would like to build. They reflected on shared outdoor spaces, gardens, how to embrace nature through their designs and the sustainability of their concepts. When outside, they began to build models of their homes. This required a relative leap in imagination which they were able to make and a small, outdoor community was created. The children gave tours of their 'homes' and created plans and 'for sale' advertisements. Sarah was satisfied that this task had given enough scope to use the outdoors, be creative but also built up their understanding of environmental factors. She was also delighted that parents were invited by the class to come and experience their new community, spending time outdoors with their children and being part of their creation.

Links to Relationships Education, Relationships and Sex Education (R(S)HE) and Health Education Statutory Guidance (2019)

Mental wellbeing

By the end of primary school:
Pupils should know:

- The benefits of physical exercise, time outdoors, community participation, voluntary and service-based activity on mental wellbeing and happiness.

Links to the PSHE Association's PSHE Education Programme of Study:

PSHE Association Core Theme 3: Living in the Wider World Key Stage 1

L5. What improves and harms their local, natural and built environments and develop strategies and skills needed to care for these (including conserving energy).

Reflection

Reflecting on the issues within Case Study 1:

- How can the local environment be incorporated into your PSHE and R(S)HE lessons? This is not restricted just to Forest school and the school grounds. It can mean using public spaces such as parks, woodlands and nature trails.
- Allowing children to be creative within a structured environment can be rewarding. How much structure would you want to give or reduce to ensure the children are able to have meaningful, outdoor experiences which are not led by the adults?
- The wonder of nature is powerful especially when tied to a meaningful experience. How many opportunities do the children in your class have to experience this?

Case Study 2: Key Stage 2

Jack's class of Year 4 children regularly receive Forest school sessions. In addition to these, he decided to develop children's understanding of risk and personal development. Creating a series of six PSHE lessons, he focused on the theme of fire. This was linked to some English work on 'No Dragons for Tea: Fire Safety for Kids (And Dragons)' and the topic of the Great Fire of London. They began by looking at reasons fire was important, how it is used and why it is dangerous. The children explored images of fires and discussed whether it was being used safely or whether or not it was a hazardous situation. Jack also discussed bushfires with the children, using recent examples from California to explore how this is managed.

Setting up a fire outside using the firepit within his Forest school area, he took his class out to watch the flames and begin to experience the heat, smells and colours associated with fire. Following this, the children were asked to start thinking about how to construct fires. The children began to build fires with different materials and setting them up in different ways. Using small flints, they practised in pairs how to spark a fire with small pieces of hay. This helped build their relationships as all of these activities involved working together. Jack modelled using the flints while discussing how to stay safe. The children then, with close monitoring, attempted the same with mixed results. Small fires were created in a controlled manner.

Links to Relationships Education, Relationships and Sex Education (R(S)HE) and Health Education Statutory Guidance (2019)

Respectful relationships

By the end of primary school:
Pupils should know:

- How to judge whether what they are feeling and how they are behaving is appropriate and proportionate.

Links to the PSHE Association's PSHE Education Programme of Study:
PSHE Association Core Theme 1: Health and wellbeing Key Stage 2

H9. To differentiate between the terms, 'risk', 'danger' and 'hazard'.
H10. To recognise, predict and assess risks in different situations and decide how to manage them responsibly.

Reflection

Reflecting on the issues within this case-study:

- Is this activity possible in your school? What is the risk threshold with staff and leadership?
- Consider how learning about fires could support their awareness of safety and managing risks in all situations.
- The wonder of nature is powerful especially when tied to a meaningful experience. How many opportunities do the children in your class have to experience this?

Some may perceive starting fires with children as a potentially risky approach especially with Key Stage 1 children. If this is not an acceptable activity in school, how can you develop children's approaches to risk in other ways? Explore the book by Mike Fairclough entitled *Playing with Fire: Embracing risk and danger in schools* for more information on how risk can be embedded in your curriculum and specifically taught in order to improve resilience for all.

Points to consider and conclusion

This chapter has argued that the outdoors is a powerful pedagogical tool that can be used to develop children's personal, social, health and relationships education. It offers multiple opportunities to deliver key aspects of the new PSHE and R(S)HE curriculum. The outdoors can often be seen as an afterthought, something that is only used when the weather is nice, yet it is an essential part of children's development, not just in the Early Years but right through their entire education. It helps their understanding of risk, develop empathy with nature and build relationships with their surroundings as well as each other. More importantly, it can help build a child's relationship with themselves; the outdoors can improve wellbeing, self-esteem and understanding of oneself, therefore must be used as frequently as possible. Recently, a colleague shared an example where the outdoors had become challenging for a Year 1 child:

One young child would always become upset when it rained. They refused to go outside for play or any activities, crying, screaming and showed extreme anxiety. This was preventing them from enjoying the outdoors and playing with others. The parents were spoken to, and it transpired that the child had been so used to putting on raincoats, waterproofs and wellies for even the slightest bit of rain, and anxiety had been built up – through no intention of the parents – about going out in the rain unless they had this 'protection'. Gradually, over time and with the parents' support, they were able to allow this child to be outside in different types of weather and experience all of the joys those environments have to offer.

This story is a warning. We must create as many opportunities to utilize the outdoors as possible for all of the children we teach, otherwise, by trying to protect them from the outdoors, we will be doing more harm than good. The outdoors is to be valued and enjoyed, especially with its impact on learning and wellbeing. Children need to 'be' outside, both physically and mentally.

Points to consider for your own setting

- What is the provision like in the outdoor settings?
- Does providing lots of tools, materials and equipment to use outdoors actually limit creativity and independent learning for children of all ages?
- How can risk be managed effectively and responsibility whilst allowing children to develop and create their own sense of risk?

Key reading

- Pickering, S. (2017), *Teaching Outdoors Creatively,* Milton: Taylor and Francis.

Further reading

- Joyce, R. (2012), Outdoor *Learning: Past and Present,* Maidenhead: Open University Press.
- Robertson, J. (2014), *Dirty Teaching: A Beginner's Guide to Learning Outdoors,* Carmarthen: Independent Thinking Press.
- White, J. (2019), *Playing and Learning Outdoors: The Practical Guide and Sourcebook for Excellence in Outdoor Provision and Practice with Young Children,* London: Routledge.

References

Christie, B., Beames, S., Higgins, P., Nicol, R. and Ross, H. (2014), 'Outdoor Learning provision in Scottish Schools', *Scottish Educational Review,* 46 (1): 48–64.

Council for Learning Outside the Classroom (2019), *Outdoor learning has huge benefits for children and teachers — so why isn't it used in more schools?* Available online: https://www.lotc.org.uk/outdoor-learning-has-huge-benefits-for-children-and-teachers-so-why-isnt-it-used-in-more-schools/ (accessed 25 October 2019).

Department for Children, Schools and Families (DfES) (2007), *The Early Years Foundation Stage – Effective Practice: Outdoor Learning.* Available online: http://outdoormatters.co.uk/wp-content/uploads/2011/03/EYFS-Effective-PracticeOutdoor-Learning.pdf (accessed 12 September 2019).

Department for Education (DfE) (2019), *Relationships Education, Relationships and Sex Education (RSE) and Health Education.* Available online: https://assets.publishing.service.gov.uk/government/uploads/system/uploads/attachment_data/file/805781/Relationships_Education__Relationships_and_Sex_Education__R(S)HE__and_Health_Education.pdf (accessed 20 November 2019).

Fairclough, M. (2016), *Playing with Fire: Embracing risk and danger in schools*, Melton: John Catt Educational Limited.

Learning and Teaching Scotland (2010), *Curriculum for Excellence Through Outdoor Learning.* Available online: https://education.gov.scot/Documents/cfe-through-outdoor-learning.pdf (accessed 25 October 2019).

Lightfoot, L. (2019), 'Forest schools: is yours more a marketing gimmick than an outdoors education?' Available online: https://www.theguardian.com/education/2019/jun/25/forest-schools-more-marketing-than-outdoor-education (accessed 1 October 2019).

Marchant, E., Todd, C., Cooksey, R., Dredge, S., Jones, H., Reynolds, D., Stratton, G., Dwyer, R., Lyons, R. and Brophy, S. (2019), 'Curriculum-based outdoor learning for children aged 9-11: A qualitative analysis of pupils' and teachers' views', *PLoS ONE*, 14 (5): 1–24.

Natural England (2016), *England's largest outdoor learning project reveals children more motivated to learn when outside.* Available online: https://www.gov.uk/government/news/englands-largest-outdoor-learning-project-reveals-children-more-motivated-to-learn-when-outside (accessed 21 October 2019).

PSHE Association (2017), *PSHE Education Programme of Study: Key Stages 1-5.* Available online: https://www.pshe-association.org.uk/curriculum-and-resources/resources/programme-study-pshe-education-key-stages-1%E2%80%935(accessed 13 September 2019).

Pendziwol, J. (1999), *No Dragons for Tea: Fire Safety for Kids (And Dragons)*, Toronto: Kids Can Press.

Robertson, J. (2014), *Dirty Teaching: A Beginner's Guide to Learning Outdoors*, Carmarthen: Independent Thinking Press.

Wildlife Trust (2019), 'New "Nature Friendly Schools" to help "green" hundreds of school grounds and bring thousands of children closer to nature'. Available online: https://www.wildlifetrusts.org/news/new-nature-friendly-schools (accessed 30 August 2019).

10

Global Learning as a Vehicle for PSHE

Elena Lengthorn and Kevin Bailey

This chapter explores:

- How global learning can bring relevance and a real context to PSHE/R(S)HE;
- The benefits of having a real context when teaching PSHE/R(S)HE;
- Some examples of how this can be done.

'Where do I fit this in?' is the familiar cry of the classroom teacher desperately balancing the demands on their ever-shrinking timetable.

Schools operate in a world of competing demands. External assessments of a narrow part of learning can lead to a further narrowing and restriction of the curriculum that does not allow creative avenues to be explored. Some of these investigative pathways may turn out to be dead ends; however, engagement in creative, open-ended enquiry supports a wide range of important learning opportunities. It is, therefore, vital that young people have this opportunity and experience the PSHE curriculum in interesting, relevant and motivating contexts.

In a fast-changing interdependent world, global learning can support and enrich learning and teaching of important concepts such as diversity and equality, human rights and fairness and justice. Personal skills and attributes such as identifying 'unhelpful' thinking traps including generalizations and stereotypes and opportunities to explore and clarify personal values can also be made relevant and meaningful. A range of interpersonal skills and attributes can also be developed: empathy and compassion; respect for others; and many skills for employability especially through a critical thinking approach. In this chapter, we will explore how aspects of global learning can be built into the curriculum using real-life contexts that also develop powerful opportunities for the enhancement of PSHE.

Global learning

Global learning – having an understanding of the issues that shape our world and connect us all, learning that furnishes pupils with the relevant knowledge, skills and values to contribute to their communities in thoughtful, ethical and responsible ways – is a core focus in PSHE. As part of the PSHE Association programme of study strand, 'Living in the Wider World' educators are encouraged to emphasize the following in core theme 3:

- To recognise that there are human rights, that they are there to protect everyone.
- About the relationship between rights and responsibilities.
- The importance of having compassion towards others; shared responsibilities we all have for caring for other people and living things; how to show care and concern for others.
- About different groups that make up their community.
- About diversity; what it means; the benefits of living in a diverse community; about valuing diversity within communities.
- About the different ways to pay for things and the choices people have about this.
- To identify the ways that money can impact on people's feelings and emotions.

PSHE Association, 2020: 18–20

The Organisation for Economic Co-operation and Development (OECD), a group of thirty-four member countries that discuss and develop economic and social policy, recognize the pressing need to prepare young people for interconnected, complex and diverse societies. Their Programme for International Student Assessment (PISA), tests fifteen year olds from all over the world, every three years, in science, maths and reading. In 2018, in recognition of rising inequalities and radicalism, the clear benefits of cooperation and connectivity and the shared vision of humanity set about in the 2015 United Nations Sustainable Development Goals (SDGs), the OECD added a further assessment framework of 'Global Competence' which they defined as:

the capacity to examine local, global and intercultural issues, to understand and appreciate the perspectives and world views of others, to engage in open, appropriate and effective interactions with people from different cultures, and to act for collective well being and sustainable development.

OECD, 2018: 7

The results of the first test in global competence will be available in December 2019 and will give us an insight into the aptitude of the world's young people in relation to:

1 Their capacity to examine issues and situations of local, global and cultural significance (e.g. poverty, migration, environmental risks);

2 The capacity to understand and appreciate different perspectives and worldviews;

3 The ability to establish positive interactions with people of different national, ethnic, religious, social or cultural backgrounds or gender; and

4 The capacity and disposition to take constructive action toward sustainable development and collective wellbeing.

OECD, 2018: 7–8

It should be noted that some key countries decided to opt out of the test, including England and the United States (Coughlan, 2018).

In order to illustrate how Global learning can be used to enhance and make relevant the PSHE curriculum we have shared two examples taken from lessons in KS1 and KS2. A brief explanation of the context and/or further information about the organizations mentioned is also included after each lesson plan.

Example lesson plan: Key Stage 1 (x 2 lessons)

Learning Objectives:

- To learn that children have rights and that everyone has responsibilities to protect those rights.
- To understand their rights (especially the right to play and rest) through the UN Convention on the Rights of the Child and their responsibilities
- To understand ways in which we are the same us others; what we have in common with everyone else.
- To help construct, and agree to follow, class rules and to understand how these rules help them.

Resources:

- Rights for Every Child (UNICEF book): https://static.unicef.org/rightsite/files/rightsforeverychild.pdf
- UN Convention on the Rights of the Child in Child Friendly Language https://static.unicef.org/rightsite/files/rights_leaflet.pdf
- Early Childhood Development Kit Activity Guide: https://www.unicef.org/videoaudio/PDFs/Activity_Guide_EnglishFINAL.pdf

- Printed images from Dollar Street (https://www.gapminder.org/dollar-street/matrix) of beds, play areas, toys and most loved toys from 'Dollar Street'.
- Camera/I-pads for taking photos.
- Access to the internet to watch one of these introductions to the UNCRC:
  What are Child Rights? By UNICEF Australia https://vimeo.com/61074030 (3:05)
  Rights of the Child Animation by the Equality and Human Rights Commission https://www.equalityhumanrights.com/en/our-human-rights-work/monitoring-and-promoting-un-treaties/convention-rights-child (3:06)
  What are Children's Rights? by The Varkey Foundation Global Teacher Prize
  https://www.youtube.com/watch?v=COjVj9czgrY (5:53)

Curriculum links:
PSHE Association Programme of Study Links (2020): L2, L3, L8, L9
R(S)HE links: Families and people who care for me, Respectful Relationships
Core themes

- About rights and responsibilities as members of families, other groups and ultimately as citizens.
- About respect for self and others and the importance of responsible behaviours and actions.
- About different groups and communities.

Global Learning Links (OECD, 2018):

- Examine issues of local, global and cultural significance (poverty, inequality, cultural difference and stereotypes).
- Understand and appreciate different perspectives and world views.
- Establish positive interactions with people of different national, ethnic, religious, social or cultural backgrounds.
- Take constructive action towards sustainable development and collective wellbeing.

Sustainable Development Goals (United Nations, 2015): 1, 3, 4 & 12.
Introduction:

1 Ask pupils individually to consider what they think a 'right' is and whether they can give an example of one. Ask them to pair share their definitions and any examples quietly with the person next to them, and then share with another pair to create groups of four pupils.

2 Invite some of the groups to share their definitions and examples to create a class definition of a 'right' on the board and compare it to a dictionary definition (e.g. a moral or legal entitlement to have or do something).

Activities:

1 Share one of the selection of 'introduction to Children's Rights' video clips (see the resources section). At the end of the clip ask them, in their groups of four, to recall as many rights as they can remember from the clip. It might be useful to collate them on a display board.

2 Connecting to their Rights:
   Prepare a jigsaw of the child-friendly version of the UNCRC (see the resources section), by dividing it into four sections, one for each pupil in the group. Invite the pupils to independently read their section and choose two or three articles that they think are the most important to share with the rest of their group.
   Or
   Select nine of the articles and give them to groups of pupils to arrange in a diamond-nine activity.
   It is crucial that pupils are encouraged to justify their thinking. Why do they think these particular rights are more important? It might also be useful to explore if there are any rights that surprised them or that they didn't understand to enable you to clarify them.

3 Discuss the outcomes of the ranking or discussion activity and invite your pupils to identify the right that they think is most important to them and why. You could invite pupils to vote using Post-it notes or a tally chart on the board. Be wary of participant social desirability bias, where they copy to please their peers rather than a share their innate feelings.

4 Remind your class that the UNCRC is more than thirty years old and share that it has become the most widely ratified human rights treaty in history, helping transform children's lives around the world. Move the discussion on to their rights in the classroom by asking them what they think their rights are in their classroom. If there is time you could break into groups and ask them to discuss or draft their own set of rights for the classroom.

5 Regroup and construct a set of class rules that would ensure that pupil rights are protected and met. Recap the rights that seemed most important or that pupils found surprising. Consider what happens if people do not know their rights? Remind/introduce pupils to UNCRC articles 42 (knowing your rights) and 31 (rest, play and culture).

Figure 4 Early Childhood Development (ECD) Box, © UNICEF.

6 Share colour images from Dollar Street of beds, play areas, toys and most loved toys from across the income range. You could ask pupils to focus on one category and either group them, arrange them by perceptions of income, or perhaps discuss them in relation to similarities and differences with their own beds, toys and play areas.

7 Share an image of a UNICEF Early Childhood Development (ECD) kit and explain:

- It is a box of toys created to strengthen the response of young children caught up in conflict or emergencies e.g. hurricanes, floods (you might link it directly to a recent emergency/conflict).
- It is designed to offer young children (aged 0–8) access to play, stimulation, learning and a sense of normalcy; it provides time for and helps children play during difficult times.
- It is very important as it creates a sense of safety, security and hope.
- The kits come with a helpful activity guide on how to use the toys based on children's ages and interests.

You might like to share some of the activity cards or even activities that are featured in the box.

8 Invite your students to create an activity card of their own for a class designed KS1 ECD kit. The children could be provided with a template and the chance to photograph or draw their favourite

activity from school or home, write a description of ways it can be played, along with what age of children the activity is designed for and a possible extension task. Swap toys with another class for another option.

Plenary:
Link your learners back to article 42 (Governments must make the Convention known to children and adults). Ask your learners, in pairs, to think of three ways we can make sure children know their rights (you might like to focus on article 31 in particular). Ask pupils how their ECD activity cards could be used to promote the right to play? Collate their ideas and consider following them up if time allows.

Next steps:
Pupils favourite ways to play ECD cards could be collated to form a KS1 Play Development Book which is shared with parents. You could share with any partner schools and swap books. Some of the favourite ways to play activities could be featured in a school event or communicated to parents via a display/ newsletter.

Background on the recommended resources

Gapminder

Gapminder is an independent Swedish foundation, a fact-tank rather than a think-tank, which has no political, religious or economic affiliations. They are on a mission to combat the massive misconceptions about global development through promoting a fact-based worldview that's easily accessible to all. The statistics they use are from collaborations with robust and reliable organizations such as the UN, Higher Education Institutions, public agencies and non-governmental organizations. Dollar Street, a resource that is highlighted in the KS1 lesson, is a Gapminder project that is free for anyone to use (they provide helpful online best-practice guidelines on how to credit their work). Dollar Street is the brainchild of Anna Rosling Ronnlund, Vice-President of Gapminder, who is passionate about the visual side of data. The project uses photos as data, enabling observers to see for themselves what life is like on different income levels all over the world. The images are from over 250 homes in fifty countries, representing basic needs such as food and water, as well as toys, pets and books.

You can test your own global misconceptions too! Gapminder invite you to take part in their straightforward Global Facts Test, freely available online. It contains thirteen questions and if you pass the test you qualify to become a 'Gapminder' and they will honour you with a Gapminder Facts Certificate! You could do this with your year or key stage teams, the whole school staff, KS2 pupils and even the wider community.

UNICEF

The aim of the United Nations International Children's Emergency Fund (UNICEF), established on 11 December 1946 by the United Nations, was to meet the emergency needs of children in post-war Europe and China. They now work to ensure the 1989 international legal framework of the United Nations Convention of the Rights of the Child (UNCRC): The world's most widely ratified human rights treaty in history is being delivered. The UK ratified in December 1991 but it has not become part of our domestic law (the content is, therefore, not legally binding).

Wide ratification has enabled more children to get the health care and nutrition they need, as well as protecting increased children from violence and exploitation. Unfortunately, the UNCRC is still not fully implemented and millions of children continue to endure violations of their rights in terms of education, health care, nutrition and safety from child marriage, conflict and dangerous work.

Using images

Our learners are living in a visual age, surrounded, bombarded even. The omnipresence of images and our engagement with them is fundamentally changing how we live and interact in the world. Photographs can be used at all levels in the classroom to offer our learners a glimpse into other people's lives across the globe, to stimulate enquiry, to question what they see and to consider perspectives and bias. We can stimulate pupils to begin considering the perspective of the photographer and their aims, to question the gaze, the cropping and the focus.

Critical thinking

In our era of ready access to information, superdiversity and increasing interdependence, it is essential that young people are capable of reviewing and categorizing the wealth of facts (and indeed fictions) at their fingertips. This requires the skills of reflective, creative and critical thinking to enable them to explore and evaluate the quality of the data that they are engaging with. The ability and confidence to 'question the given'.

Snyder and Snyder (2008) champion the learnability of critical thinking and suggest these are skills that should be practised continually, that they require active learning opportunities and good modelling from teachers. Criticality is not innate and pupils may not have had experiences that required evaluative thought previously. Ruggiero (2012) identified seven key critical thinking characteristics that include: acknowledging knowledge limits; considering problems and controversial issues as exciting and challenging; showing an interest in the ideas of others; recognizing that extreme views are rarely correct; and to practice fair mindedness, as well as thinking before acting. Global learning, as part of your PSHE curriculum, offers many problems and controversial topics for consideration and the development of your pupil's critical thinking skills.

With practise, these essential criticality skills can be embedded into all PSHE curriculum areas and help pupils avoid an overdramatic worldview and instead formulate views based on facts. This factful approach will help our learners stress less about the wrong things and make better decisions about real dangers and possibilities (Rosling, 2018).

Reflection

What is a right? This can be a challenging concept for young children. What 'rights' might children best relate to in order to begin this conversation?

The following lesson ideas will invite pupils to connect with their rights and responsibilities as a child both within and beyond their classroom. These activities could contribute to the UNICEF Rights Respecting Schools Award (UNICEF, 2019) by putting the UNCRC into practice.

'Intouch Gambia' is an organization working in the smallest mainland country in Africa, The Gambia. Their vision is to support access to high-quality solar lamps so that traditional methods of lighting such as candles, oil lamps and torches can be reduced to the minimum. Solar lights are distributed to rural, off-grid schools and rented to pupils on a weekly basis for the cost of a candle. Solar committees made up of teachers and community members manage the scheme and aim to develop confidence in solar energy as an alternative to expensive, unhealthy and more dangerous alternatives. Profit from the programme enable schools to reinvest in replacement lamps and to grow the solar library to enable more students to have access to lamps. A small shop based in the community gives a point of purchase if requested and payment schemes are available should community members find 'one off' payment difficult to afford.

Figure 5 Solar lamps being used in Faraba, The Gambia, for an evening study group.

Example Lesson Plans: Key Stage 2

Learning Objectives:

- To understand the significance of easy access to electricity.
- To understand how access to electricity varies across the world.
- To evaluate a sustainable project which gives communities access to affordable solar lighting.
- To understand that access to power is a basic human need.

Resources:

- British Council units – 'Affordable, Clean Energy for All'.
- Know, wonder, learned (KWL) chart.
- 'Dollar Street' (https://www.gapminder.org/dollar-street/matrix>).
- Printed images of lights from 'Dollar Street'.
- 'Switched On Gambia' website (https://switchedon-gambia.weebly.com/).

- Intouch Gambia (www.intouchgambia.org).
- https://www.tidegloballearning.net/primary-early-years/talking-about-photographs

PSHE Association Programme of Study Links (2020): L2, L3, L4, L5, L18, L19, L20
R(S)HE links: Families and people who are for me & Respectful relationships

- About rights and responsibilities as members of families, other groups and ultimately as citizens.
- That families either in school or the wider world sometimes look different from their family, but they should respect those differences.
- About respect for self and others and the importance of responsible behaviours and actions.
- About different groups and communities.

Global Learning Links (OECD, 2018):

- Examine issues of local, global and cultural significance (poverty, inequality, cultural difference and stereotypes).
- Understand and appreciate different perspectives and worldviews.
- Establish positive interactions with people of different national, ethnic, religious, social or cultural backgrounds.
- Take constructive action towards sustainable development and collective wellbeing.

Sustainable Development Goals (United Nations, 2015): 1, 3, 4, 7, 8, 11, 12 and 13

Lesson 1

Introduction:

1 In pairs or small groups, ask students to answer the question 'What do you already know about electricity?'
2 Then ask them 'What do you want to find out?' Record their responses using a KWL Chart.
3 Keep for later reflection.

Activities:

1 In pairs ask students to consider basic human needs for survival.
2 Share them with another pair and agree on five ideas. Write on separate pieces of paper.
3 Share with whole class by placing in piles with similar ideas.
4 Place ideas in two groups. One that needs or would be improved with electricity and one that would not need electricity.

5 Introduce 'Dollar Street' and search on the topic of 'light sources'.

6 Consider the variety of lights and the energy used.

Plenary:

In small groups sort a selection of photographs into two piles. Those that use electricity and those that don't. Share results.

Lesson 2

Introduction:

1 Introduce the organizations 'Switched On Gambia' and 'Intouch Gambia' using their website.

2 Discuss the principle aims of the project and why they are important.

3 Refer back to the first lesson and how access to electricity supports basic human needs.

4 Connect with the lesson on 'Rights'. Can this project support any of those 'rights'?

Activities:

1 Give class information on costs of candles in The Gambia (currently 10 pence per candle).

2 Compare with price of a simple high-quality solar light (currently approximately £3). Calculate how long it would take to purchase a solar light if this money could be saved.

3 What are the advantages of owning a solar light?

Plenary:

Set up a 'hot seat' activity with a child taking the part of a Gambian mother or father who would like a solar lamp. Class ask questions to investigate why.

Reflection

'What happens to solar lamps when they stop working and can no longer be repaired?'

This is an interesting question to ask. Many children will suggest putting in the bin or even the recycling bin but what if the infrastructure is non-existent? What is the environmental impact? How would that compare with candles and batteries?

Points to consider and conclusion

We hope that these examples of lessons illustrate how Global Learning can set real contexts for the development of thinking about many aspects of the PSHE/R(S)HE curriculum that takes young people beyond their immediate classroom, and personal relationships, and gives them an opportunity to reflect on wider global issues.

Points to consider for your own setting

- Does the curriculum in your school allow for PSHE/R(S)HE and global learning to be taught together?
- Does your school allow access to the recommended online resources? E.g. www.Gapminder.org

---

Key reading

- The British Council (2020) *Connecting Classrooms through Global Learning.* Available online: https://connecting-classrooms.britishcouncil.org/sites/default/files/education_for_sustainable_development_and_global_citizenship_resource.pdf (accessed 19 May 2020).
- OXFAM (2019) *The Sustainable Development Goals: A guide for teachers.* Available online: https://policy-practice.oxfam.org.uk/publications/the-sustainable-development-goals-a-guide-for-teachers-620842?pscid=ps_ggl_gr_Google+Grants+-+Policy%26Practice+-+DSA_Policy+%26+Practice&gclid=CjwKCAjwkun1BRAIEiwA2mJRWQuPIEpL0DyEGnzmlpJCDozYBNMNEzAE8JmwrejqiEeK2QpdeLr7GxoC9sMQAvD_BwE&gclsrc=aw.ds (accessed 19 May 2020).

Further reading

- Gapminder (no date) A *Teachers Guide to Factfulness.* Available online: https://www.gapminder.org/wp-content/uploads/Factfulness-Teachers-Guide-Eng-181010.pdf (accessed 19 May 2020).
- Quijada, A. (2013), *Developing Critical Creating critical thinkers through media literacy.* Available online: https://www.youtube.com/watch?v=aHAApvHZ6XE (accessed 19 May 2020).

- My Rights Passport by Amnesty International. Available to order online: https://www.amnesty.org.uk/resources/my-rights-passport

References

Coughlan, S. (2018), 'England and US will not take Pisa tests in tolerance'. BBC.

OECD (2018), *Teaching for Global Competence in a Rapidly Changing World*, Available online: https://www.oecd.org/education/teaching-for-global-competence-in-a-rapidly-changing-world-9789264289024-en.htm (accessed 12 May 2020).

PSHE Association (2020), *Programme of Study for PSHE Education: Key Stages 1-4*, Available online: https://www.pshe-association.org.uk/curriculum-and-resources/resources/programme-study-pshe-education-key-stages-1%E2%80%935 (accessed 12 May 2020).

Rosling, H. Rosling, O. and Rosling-Runnland, A. (2018), *Factfulness: ten reasons we're wrong about the world – and why things are better than you think*, Flatiron Books: New York.

Ruggiero, V. R. (2012), *The art of thinking: A guide to critical and creative thought*, 10th edn, New York: Longman.

Snyder, L. G. and Snyder, M. J. (2008), 'Teaching Critical Thinking and Problem-Solving Skills', *The Delta Pi Epsilon Journal*, 1 (2): 90–9.

United Nations (2015), *About the Sustainable Development Goals*. Available online: https://www.un.org/sustainabledevelopment/sustainable-development-goals/ (accessed 12 May 2020).

11

The Movement of People
and PSHE

Elena Lengthorn and Ann Russell

This chapter explores:

- Fun, interactive, activities with a focus on refugees and migration;
- The importance of teaching about refugees and migration within PSHE;
- Human Rights and our individual responsibilities.

'Big numbers!' says the six-year-old. 'So what!' says another. Yet the numbers are so relevant for understanding the enormity of the current worldwide crisis. How can a young child grasp the gravity of these statistics? Please refer to Figure 6 overleaf.

The numbers highlight that we are living in a world changing for a variety of reasons and as people move, their movement will impact on the communities in which they settle. What a diverse and confusing world young children face! A principle of PSHE teaching is to teach children in the here and now, in context and reality. Since the Second World War there have been many events which have led to the dispersal of people. For example, the establishment of the independent states of India and Pakistan (1947) led to 14 million refugees, the Hungarian Uprising (1956) 200,000 refugees, the Czechoslovakian uprising (1968) 80,000 refugees and the expulsion of Ugandan Asians by Idi Amin (1972) 27,000 refugees. Long-forgotten and the effects of migration now absorbed by the communities, these and many other events show that migration is not a new phenomenon. However the world is currently in the midst of the greatest movement of people in contemporary history. Migrants and refugees regularly make the headlines, often with a portrayal of the negative effects of migration alongside the arrival of refugees. Children are being exposed to

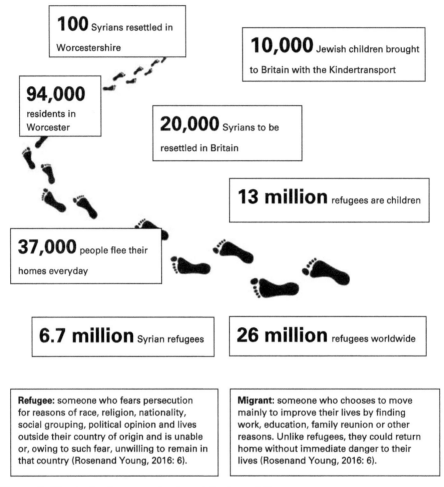

Figure 6 Chart of refugee and migrant facts and figures.

the reality of this crisis on a regular basis, whether or not there are refugee children in their own school. This is therefore a real issue for children and cannot be sidelined for being controversial or political. Teachers have a responsibility to respond.

By law, under The Equality Act 2010, schools must eliminate unlawful discrimination, promote equality of opportunity, and promote good relations between people from different groups, including those from different ethnic backgrounds. The PSHE Programme of Study for KS2 specifically introduces the teaching of the United Nations Declaration of the Rights of the Child. The Teacher Standards Part 2 also endorse the showing of tolerance and respect for the rights of others.

More pertinent however is the response of the PSHE Association that declares: 'It is not enough to simply teach pupils *about* the issues covered in the suggested subject content. It is vital they have the opportunity to explore their attitudes, values and beliefs about them and to develop the skills, language and strategies necessary to *manage* these issues should they encounter them in their lives.' (PSHE Association, 2017: 5). These issues of equality, promotion of good relations between people, human rights and the responsibility to protect those rights are also often considered to be controversial but are specifically covered in the PSHE Association Programme of Study as part of Living in the Wider World, and in the new R(S)HE curriculum in 'Caring Relationships', 'Respectful relationships' and 'Families and people who care for me'. The teaching of PSHE and R(S)HE provides a way to challenge perceptions and to promote understanding and acceptance, good relations between people from different groups and ethnic backgrounds. It endorses the critical examination of the topical, if controversial, events of the world which are being presented in the home, in the press and social media and can do so in a safe and supportive environment, equipping the children with the skills, language and strategies to navigate, participate and thrive in the modern world.

Try this

Take a grain of rice. Each grain of rice represents a very special person – YOU. A very powerful picture can be made and statistics brought to life as a pile of rice, the grains of which all represent a special person just like you, tells a story about humanity. Refugee information can be shared with statistics about your school, local community, football clubs, etc. and children can start to think and question how the world is organized (Stan's Café Theatre, 2003).

Grounding teaching in the United Nations Convention on The Rights of the Child (United Nations, 1989), any teaching content on refugee and migrant issues can be related to the appropriate Rights as a starting point for teacher planning. Then start with a story. The UK has a plethora of children's books, authors and illustrators who capture the imagination of young people and can take them on a learning journey far beyond the classroom. There are many books reflecting on migration and refugees, and the universality of human rights (see Children's books at the end of the chapter). From the pupil's perspective it is helpful to start with ideas children can relate to and have their own experience of. Homes and journeys are two common topics in the Early Years and Primary curricula. By sharing common experiences, young children will begin to develop an understanding of how much they have in common with children whose experiences are very different to their own, and begin to grow in empathy with those same children. As adults they should be able to embrace the common humanity they share rather than build walls and bridges between each other.

Try this

Display a child-friendly poster of the Rights of a Child. Make cards of a selection of Rights and ask children to order them in priority. Compare how each child or group orders them. Remind children that these are Rights for all children and there is no right or wrong order. Children could make their own cards illustrating a Right they have chosen. Display in class or in public areas as a reminder to everyone of their shared humanity. Find a child-friendly version of the UNCRC here: https://www.slideshare.net/fawhs/un-convention-on-the-rights-of-the-child-in-child-friendly-language-13905511

Figure 7 A picture of home: Ritsona Camp, Greece, August 2016. Photo by Chris Russell.

Lesson Plan: KS1

Learning Objectives:

- To consider what home means.
- To show empathy with children who have been forced to leave their homes.

Resources:

- The story of The Three Little Pigs.
- Paper and crayons, pencils or colouring pens.
- film – Amal's Story: bit.ly/Amal-story or direct link https://app. aframe.com/links/2ba20b3814e9d2f92fff59911f3605cc

Curriculum links:

PSHE Association Programme of Study Links (2020): H11, H14, R23, L5, L6

RSE curriculum (2019) : Families and People who care for me, Respectful relationships

SDG (United Nations, 2015): 16.3

Introduction:
Make a class list of what home means.

Activity 1:
Watch Amal's story. Explain that more than half the world's refugees are children. Imagine half the class having to flee from their homes. Discuss what you think Amal felt about her home? What about after she had been forced to leave? What do you think she thought home was like in the refugee camp? Imagine living in a refugee camp. Record ideas as a class list.

Activity 2:
In small groups retell the story of The Three Little Pigs. Divide the class into three groups – instead of three pigs there are three groups of children – one group lives in a house of straw, one in a house of sticks, one in a house of bricks. Each child draws their house. Ask children to stand together in their groups then retell the story so it becomes The Three Little Children. When the wolf blows down the straw house, take away the children's drawings. They now have nowhere to live. Their houses have been destroyed. One of this group goes and asks the stick houses group if they can come and live with them (they may need some encouragement). The straw house children then join the stick house children. The same process happens when the wolf has destroyed the stick houses and they must live with the brick house children. All the children will now be huddled together in one space, sharing the brick houses.

Ask the children how they felt being forced out of their homes (some had to move twice), and ask those who took others in how it felt to share their space. Record responses.

Plenary:
Look at the original list of what home means. How much changes if you are forced out of your home? Compare ideas from the Introduction and Activities 1 and 2.

Extension ideas:
Literacy – Create a word bank for feelings for the different sections of the story. Create an emotions graph showing where some of the words would be placed.

Figure 8 Home is where your Mom is. Photo by Yannis Behrakis.

Images such as this are a valuable tool for stimulating discussion and developing critical thinking skills.

Reflection on KS1 lesson plan

What makes home?
Where is it? What does it mean? All children will have ideas of what home means to them and this will help young learners to identify with other people. With millions of people on the move, home may take on a new look.

Reflect on the photo in Fig. 8. *Where do you think it was taken? Who do you think took it? How does it make you feel? Where is your home? What would your slogan be to describe your sense of home?*

It is important to remember that an understanding of the lives and families of your pupils is essential in order to be sensitive when exploring issues of 'home'.

Journeys

'Are we nearly there yet?' Who hasn't heard that refrain on a journey? Where did you go? How long was the journey? What did you pack? Even if a child's only experience of a journey is the journey to school, every child can relate to a journey. With millions on the move within and across borders, the stories of journeys can take on a completely new look.

Lesson Plan: KS2

Learning Objective:

- To develop empathy with refugee children; to consider difficult choices.

Resources:

- World map or map showing route Syria-Germany.
- Picture of refugee family: https://www.worldvision.org/refugees-news-stories/syrian-refugee-google-map-perspective
- Child's rucksack with change of clothes, passport, money, first aid kit, toy, precious object.
- Outline of rucksack for each child.

Curriculum links:
PSHE Association Programme of Study Links (2020): R32, R33, L4, L9
RSE curriculum (2019) : Families and People who care for me, Respectful relationships
SDG (United Nations, 2015): 16.3

Introduction:
Let's make music! Clap hands if you came to school by car; tap your head if you came by bus; snap your fingers if you cycled; slap your thighs if you walked.

Discuss what type of journeys the children make. Together make a list of what they would pack for a holiday.

Activity 1:
Look at another journey. Show a map showing the journey from Syria to Europe. Highlight that this journey is about 1,400 miles, 50 days walking for 8 hours a day covering 25 miles a day. Show picture of a refugee family travelling. Thumb thermometers – 'Is it right this family and the other 12 million should be forced to leave their homes?' Thumb thermometers – 'Is it right that this family and more than 12 million should be allowed to a life of freedom and safety?'

Activity 2:
Hold up a pre-packed rucksack. Tell the children they have had to leave home in a hurry and do not know if they will return. What would you pack? Give each child an outline of a rucksack. Children draw or write in the outline what they would pack – remind them they have to carry this themselves.

Look at the drawings and share ideas. Look at the contents of the packed rucksack and compare with the packing of the children. Who has a passport, money, first aid kit? Who packed a small toy to prevent boredom? Who packed a teddy for comfort.? Are these the things you packed for your holiday at the beginning of the lesson?

Then ask what they would choose if they could only carry items in their coat pockets.

Plenary:
Discuss why children made the choices they did. What have they learnt about the life and choices of a refugee child?

Extension ideas:
Literacy – read *The Journey* by Francesca Sanna. Use this as a stimulus for story writing. Swap places with the characters in the story – what are your feelings, hopes, needs, etc.? Look at an old rucksack. What stories of travels could it tell? Look at a well-worn shoe. Who did it belong to? Where has it been? What stories could it tell?

Reflection

Controversy and politics

Do not be afraid to tackle controversial and political ideas, they are part of everyday life. If children are not introduced to the events of the world, their understanding of the world becomes correspondingly limited. By becoming familiar with contemporary issues relating to inequality, and justice on local and global levels, children will discover a range of ideas about solutions, and be better placed to acknowledge other viewpoints and opinions. The education process should transform society, and PSHE should equip children to think about others and be empowered to take action based on evidence, emotional and intellectual factors.

Consider this:

- Is there a school that does not get involved with Red Nose Day or Comic Relief Day? How do you explain to a child why they are having a cake sale if the social, moral and often controversial concerns that lay behind the fundraising are not discussed?
- Look beyond fund raising to believing you can become part of the change. See 'Points to consider and conclusion'.

As PSHE covers the health and wellbeing of children, the learning of confidence and building up of self-esteem, it is pertinent to consider the health and wellbeing of refugees and migrants after they have been resettled in places of safety.

2018 marked the twentieth anniversary of Refugee Week and amidst the celebrations there was the opportunity to celebrate the huge contributions refugees and migrants have made to their new communities. The hardships and traumas they encountered as they left one life to start another is only part of the story, and it is important not to let young children remain with the negative feelings about what refugees face, but encourage them look to the future, a future of hope and success.

Try this

What do the people in Table 7) have in common? As you finish a scheme of work about refugees and migrants, play a final game to let children find out about people or celebrities they know of but did not realize their backgrounds. You may be surprised. You never know, someone near you may also have such a story to tell. There are some useful resources here: https://refugeeweek.org.uk/resources/facts-figures-and-contributions/famous-refugees/

Table 7 Table of refugees and their achievements

	Michael Marks, a Polish Jewish refugee, arrived in Britain around 1882. He became one of the founders of the chain store Marks and Spencer.
	Judith Kerr arrived in Britain in 1933, aged ten years old, to escape Nazi Germany. She is famous for her book about this experience, *When Hitler Stole Pink Rabbit* but even more famous for her picture book, *The Tiger Who Came to Tea*.
	Malala Yousafzai came to Britain in 2012 aged fifteen. She had been shot in the head by the Taliban in Pakistan for standing up for the right to education. She is the co-recipient of the 2014 Nobel Peace Prize and is now studying at Oxford University.
	Mounzer al-Darsani, from Damascus, Syria arrived in Bute in 2016. He has successfully integrated into the community, and is now running his own barber shop.
	Yusra Mardini, was fifteen when she and her sister left Syria in 2015. To save the over-loaded dinghy she and her sister were in, they had to swim in the sea, steering it to safety. A year later she swam for the Refugee Olympic Athlete Team and is now training in Germany for the 2020 Olympics.
	Amineh Abou Kerech was thirteen when she arrived in England from Syria in 2017. She spoke no English but ten months after her arrival won the Betjeman Poetry Prize with her poem, *Lament for Syria*.

Points to consider and conclusion

When a school ethos reflects an understanding and positive response to refugees and migrants, there is a greater chance that this will be reflected in a growing child. Just as it is not enough to simply teach about the issues covered, schools should look forward and consider what action the school community can take. There are many ways to respond. Celebrate World Refugee Day, Human Rights Day, International Day of the Child, Holocaust Day. Invite a speaker from an NGO or charity to lead an assembly or workshop so that children learn what those organizations are doing, what can be done, and how they too can become agents of change, and not merely fundraisers. Social Action is indeed highlighted in the RSE curriculum under Paragraph 60. For an embedded approach to ensuring human rights becomes entrenched in the school ethos, schools can consider becoming a School of Sanctuary or Rights Respecting School.

'I feel like an evacuee', a resident of Whaley Bridge, Derbyshire told a reporter in June 2019, following the evacuation of the village due to the instability of the reservoir structure as a result of unseasonal weather. Could this be the result of climate change in Britain? This is not the chapter to discuss that topic further but it does reinforce that the need to migrate can affect anyone, anywhere, including places much closer to home. Climate change could become an even more major player in migration sometime in the future. Learning today about the effects of migration will empower children to tackle migration issues in the future.

Points to consider for your own setting

- Do staff have access to a range of resources and stories to support teaching about refugees and migration? There is a useful online list here: https://www.booktrust.org.uk/booklists/b/books-about-refugees-and-asylum-seekers-younger-children/
- Consider carrying out an audit to assess how 'rights and respecting' your school is. You could use the UNICEF tools here: https://www.unicef.org.uk/rights-respecting-schools/resources/teaching-resources/rrsa-forms-and-guides/bronze-forms-guides/
- What next? How about inviting key organizations to contribute to your school programme? You could explore how to become a UNICEF Rights Respecting School (https://www.unicef.org.uk/rights-respecting-schools/) or a 'School of Sanctuary' (https://schools.cityofsanctuary.org/).

Key reading

- Claire, H. (2001), *Not aliens: Primary School children and the citizenship/PSHE curriculum,* Stoke on Trent: Trentham Books.
  This book is about everyone's right to citizenship and the right for children to have their voice heard in the adult world. Chapter 6 is particularly important covering values in education and offers a framework for children to work with ideas about justice, rights and responsibilities, care and compassion.
- Oxfam (2018), *Managing controversial issues.* Available online: https://policy-practice.oxfam.org.uk/publications/teaching-controversial-issues-a-guide-for-teachers-620473 (accessed 19 May 2020).
  A very user-friendly resource pack with photos, video links and activities.
- UNICEF (2020), *In Search of Safety: Teaching about Europe's Refugee Crisis.* Available online: https://www.unicef.org.uk/rights-respecting-schools/resources/teaching-resources/refugee-crisis-europe/ (accessed 19 May 2020).

 # Further reading: Children's books

- Amnesty International (2008), *We Are All Born Free,* London: Frances Lincoln.
  The Universal Declaration of Human Rights in Pictures with contributions from well-known children's illustrators such as Axel Scheffler and Chris Riddell.
- Gratz, A. (2017), *Refuge,* London: Scholastic Ltd. (Recommended for Upper KS2)
  This book tells the story of three children who embark on harrowing journeys in search of refuge. The children; one Jewish, escaping from Nazi Germany; one Cuban escaping riots and unrest; one Syrian, leaving a homeland torn apart by violence, preparing for a long trek toward Europe, all face unimaginable dangers, yet cling to the hope of tomorrow.
- Milner, K. (2017), *My Name is not Refugee,* Edinburgh: The Bucket List.
  A well written and powerfully illustrated picture book encouraging empathy about the plight of many children leaving home in search of safety. Discussion points on every page encourage readers to put themselves in another's shoes. What would you take? How far can you walk?
- Sanna, F. (2016), *The Journey,* London: Flying Eye Books.
  Through beautiful and powerful illustrations, *The Journey* tells the story of what a refugee family goes through to reach a safe place.
- UNICEF (2000), *For Every Child,* London: Hutchinson Children's Books.
  This book promotes the UN Convention on the Rights of a Child, illustrating fourteen of the fifty-four rights. The pictures are extremely clear and can be used independently to encourage thinking and discussion.

Further reading

- *First News* – an award-winning national newspaper for children, presenting current affairs and politics in a child friendly format.

References

PSHE Association (2017), *PSHE Association Programme of Study*. Available online: https://www.pshe-association.org.uk/system/files/PSHE%20Education%20 Programme%20of%20Study%20%28Key%20stage%201-5%29%20Jan%202017_2.pdf (accessed 1 October 2019).

PSHE Association (2020), *Programme of Study for PSHE Education: Key Stages 1-4*. Available online: https://www.pshe-association.org.uk/curriculum-and-resources/ resources/programme-study-pshe-education-key-stages-1%E2%80%935 (accessed on 12 May 2020).

Rosen, M. and Young, A. (2016), *Who are Refugees and Migrants? What makes people leave their homes? And Other Big Questions,* London: Wayland Books.

Stan's Café Theatre (2003), *Of all the people in all the world*. Available online: http://www.stanscafe.co.uk/project-of-all-the-people.html (accessed 1 October 2019).

Tagaris, K. (2017), 'Refugees brave snow, sub-zero temperatures in Greek camps', *Reuters*, 10 January. Available online: https://uk.reuters.com/article/uk-europe-migrants-greece-snow/refugees-brave-snow-sub-zero-temperatures-in-greek-camps-idUKKBN14U28V (accessed on 1 October 2019).

United Nations (2015), *About the Sustainable Development Goals*. Available online: https://www.un.org/sustainabledevelopment/sustainable-development-goals/ (accessed 12 May 2020).

United Nations General Assembly, Convention on the Rights of the Child, 20 November 1989, United Nations, Treaty Series

12

Supporting Children's Mental Health through PSHE and R(S)HE

Suzanne Allies

This chapter explores:

- The core theme of Health and Wellbeing as recommended by the PSHE Association (2020) and R(S)HE guidance, as specified by the DfE (2019);
- How you can deliver your wellbeing lessons in order that you can confidently and sensitively facilitate discussions about mental health with your class;
- Two PSHE lesson ideas to model good practice.

High-quality PSHE and R(S)HE teaching ensures that a child's happiness, and physical and mental health, is being prioritized and reflected upon by teachers, caregivers and children themselves. The content in lessons should enhance and complement the wellbeing provision already being provided by a school and teaching needs to expose children to a variety of skills that stem from possessing sound mental health, such as resilience and empathy. With repetition, these skills ideally will become habitual to children so they will unconsciously integrate them into their everyday lives. With good mental health, or mental wealth, children are more able to battle and accept life's lows and achieve their full academic potential. The research findings and recommendations from the Education Endowment Foundation (2020) highlight the importance of social and emotional learning and its contribution to achievement and attainment. They recommend teaching staff to 'integrate and model

Social and Emotional Learning (SEL) skills through everyday teaching' and to 'Reinforce SEL skills through whole-school ethos and activities' (Education Endowment Foundation, 2020: 1).

Delivering content, related to health and wellbeing, should not be a daunting prospect for teachers. Only the most basic of knowledge is required, without any expectation to be an expert in mental health. First and foremost, it is necessary for a teacher to simply reflect upon their school's unique circumstances; this reflection will ensure that lesson planning relates specifically to their desired teaching style and the context and values of a school and its community, as advised by the Department for Education (2019) and the PSHE Association (2020). Using a spontaneous and flexible approach, will allow PSHE learning to be personal, meaningful and memorable.

This chapter begins by addressing the wider context of children's mental health by mentioning current statistics and recent government guidance. The perspective then narrows to stress the importance of a whole-school wellbeing approach and then narrows further as the remaining information deals directly with the individual teacher and how health and wellbeing lessons can be planned. Wherever possible, however, it is useful to encourage collaboration between teachers in a school when addressing challenging PSHE topics. Pairing up with other teachers can be extremely useful so that learning is being facilitated confidently and in a supportive and holistic way. Furthermore, it may be worth considering the involvement of outside speakers, as the PSHE Association (2019) suggest. However, be conscious to select speakers carefully and liaise with them during, and prior to, the visit so they address topics in an appropriate way for your class.

Current statistics related to the mental health of children in England

You may be thinking: Why would I discuss depression with a child in Key Stage 1 or 2? Your opinion may be that they are too young for this subject matter. PSHE and R(S)HE need to embrace the complicated and more sensitive issues that are a reality of our world (Woolley, 2010).

Sadly, it has been found that one in four girls have depression by the time they are fourteen years old, as shown by Patalay and Fitzsimons (2016); this study was extensive and involved the questionnaires and interviews of more than 10,000 children aged fourteen. Findings indicate therefore, that the mental health education of our children is urgently required, alongside early intervention from mental health services. Indeed, figures in 2017 indicted that 12.8 per cent (or 1 in 8) of children aged five to nineteen and 5.5 per cent of children aged between two to four years, had experienced at least one mental disorder (National Health Service, 2018). It has been estimated that approximately 150,000 of our UK children in mainstream and special schools are suffering from Social, Emotional and Mental Health (SEMH) needs.

The wider perspective

If you have been allocated a role in school to support the mental health of children, such as Designated Mental Health Lead (DMHL), then a plethora of government papers exist on the www.gov.uk website that will prove to be invaluable in informing your decisions (please see 'Key reading' and 'Further reading' sections below). For example, on page 8 of 'Mental Health and Behaviour in Schools' (DfE, 2014, updated Nov. 2018) you can learn about mental health risk factors in a school, such as bullying, and mental health protective factors in a school, such as pupils having a sense of belonging. These will provide you with an overall idea of the part that a school can play in supporting positive mental health.

The document that I particularly wish to point out, as it contains a variety of useful advice and guidance, is a PSHE Association paper funded by the DfE called *Teacher guidance: teaching about mental health and emotional wellbeing* (updated for 2019). This document has been designed to increase the confidence of teachers in the delivery of wellbeing lessons. The PSHE Association recognize that teachers may find it 'challenging' (PSHE Association, 2019: 5) to teach about mental health, especially as it is very likely that children will be 'affected by the issues being addressed'. As a supplement to this document, the PSHE Association (2020) have mapped the current Programmes of Study to the guidance, to enable your content to be fully up to date.

Reflection

What do I need to consider prior to teaching?

- Which skills should I be teaching my class of pupils to encourage them to thrive and become happier, more contented individuals?
- Which topics seem most pertinent? These could include anxiety, depression, self-harm, bereavement, social media and body image issues.
- What prior knowledge exists? This information will allow you to pitch the lesson content appropriately and in the most meaningful way for individuals and as a collective.

- How can I ensure that links are made explicit between lessons and learning is extended?
- Which ground rules will I establish for these lessons? The PSHE Association (2019:6–8) emphasize that rules need to be 'negotiated and agreed with pupils'. They stress to make sure that issues are discussed sensitively whilst encouraging a positive classroom climate, atmosphere and positive shared language. Rules centring around the following are recommended: listening to each other without judgement and without assumptions, openness, the right to pass and using a non-judgemental approach. They highlight confidentiality amongst peers, but for the teacher to explain details about when they would need to break confidentiality.

Encouraging a whole-school approach to wellbeing

It is crucial to maintain a whole-school approach to teaching mental health and wellbeing. I recommend that teachers share wellbeing insights gained, about the children in their class, with the DMHL. If any children require assistance, then ideally you would collaborate with the DMHL or SENCo about accessing support for them.

The main reason for adopting a whole-school approach is because there is tremendous power in collective messages aimed at addressing any mental health misconceptions, discrimination or stigma. If a school's ethos, and the attitude of staff, is consistently positive and supportive of pupils with mental health needs then this feeling will spread and translate to everyone associated with the school. For instance, if every teacher encourages openness and honest discussions about mental health then this will become the norm and mental health will be considered in a similar vein and prioritized equally to physical health.

Although the above mental health figures for children suggest the doom and gloom of mental ill health for children, it is important that a school maintains an optimistic outlook and shares supportive strategies and protective factors. Nevertheless, it is still crucial to discuss unhealthy coping mechanisms with children.

Reflection

What is meant by the term 'mental health' and what does a mentally healthy child look like?

The dictionary definition of mental health is 'A state of emotional and psychological well-being in which an individual is able to use his or her cognitive and emotional capabilities, function in society, and meet the ordinary demands of everyday life.'

Children need to appreciate that everyone's mental health and moods fluctuate on a daily basis. Children may wish to draw a line on a whiteboard to show where they feel their mental health has risen and fallen that day. This will allow them to see how their mood will dip and soar according to how they are feeling and what has been happening to them. As highlighted by the DfE (2019) children need to appreciate how physical and mental health are interlinked.

The Mental Health Foundation (2002) lists the child characteristics that are exemplary of good mental health. They state that a child will typically:

- Develop psychologically, emotionally, intellectually and spiritually.
- Initiate, develop and sustain mutually satisfying personal relationships.
- Use and enjoy solitude.
- Become aware of others and empathize with them.
- Play and learn.
- Develop a sense of right and wrong.
- Resolve (face) problems and setbacks and learn from them.

Key Stage 1 lesson: Loss

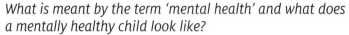

Death is an uncomfortable subject for many, but we should encourage children to voice their feelings about death and most specifically about all the types of loss that they have encountered and their individual response. When I use the term loss, I refer, for example, to the ending or change in a friendship, the break-up of their family and the death of a pet or person. After the COVID-19 pandemic, teachers will need to be extra vigilant in recognizing how change, transition and loss are being coped with by youngsters should any of them need support. After all, this situation and the sudden closure of our schools, has highlighted the unpredictability and uncertainty involved in life. As much as is possible, we need to encourage our children to adapt and gain an acceptance of inevitable change.

Here is an example of how an empathic and caring teacher deals with the sensitive subject of loss:

Lesson context and setting:

Clare has a Year 1 class. The month is May and so Clare knows her pupils well. She particularly relishes incorporating PSHE elements into the curriculum wherever it is most appropriate. She has just qualified and gained a certificate in Level 2 counselling skills having studied part-time for a year. Therefore, Clare has honed and practised effective active listening skills and finds them exceptionally useful to facilitate discussions about mental health and wellbeing with the children, some of whom are quite introverted. This lesson has been designed in response to a need she identified in her class. Six children have experienced a significant loss since Christmas and Clare is concerned about their wellbeing and emotional state owing to this:

- One child has experienced the death of their family dog who died traumatically from a road traffic accident.
- One child has experienced the separation and imminent divorce of their parents.
- One child has lost their father to suicide.
- One child has recently moved to a new house.
- One child has moved schools and subsequently lost many friends.
- One child's grandparent died after battling cancer.

The setting for this activity is in the outdoor forest area. There has been extensive research, such as that commissioned by Natural England (2016) that emphasizes the physical and mental health benefits of children spending time outdoors. Clare's headteacher has made it a policy that every class spends at least one day per week learning outside of the classroom. Clare commented that this has had a very positive impact upon children's wellbeing and staff morale and wellbeing.

Previously, children have produced pictures in an art lesson depicting their feelings when they lose someone, or an object, that they love. Clare analysed her pupil's pictures for signs of mental distress and thereby concluded that investigating the theme of loss in more depth with these children would be beneficial. She is conscious that concepts need to be revisited, reinforced and extended.

Hide and Seek task:

Clare hides pictures and words around the theme of mental health in the forest school area. For example, there is a picture of a cloud, a child crying and a child hugging their pet dog, and words such as 'lonely', 'worried' and 'excited'. Children are instructed to sit on a log when they find a card; the class know that this encourages fairness and teamwork. With assistance from the TA, every child attaches their card to a wall and a class discussion is stimulated. For example, a picture of a child their age crying, and a picture of an adult crying encourages a discussion about what it feels like to cry and whether it is acceptable to cry anywhere. One child insists that 'grown-ups' should not cry as this is 'scary'. Clare explains it is normal for anyone, irrespective of their age, to feel sad and that crying is a natural and normal response to sadness. 'My dad never cries,' says one child and the child whose father had died by suicide shares: 'My dad always cried'. Clare signals subtlety to the TA to approach this child and monitor him for the rest of the lesson. Clare selects the words 'loss', 'change', 'grief' and 'adapt' and asks the children to interpret the meaning of them and whether the words have anything in common. One child says: 'They are all about when someone dies.' Clare responds: 'Does the word "change" just have to do with when someone dies?' She parrots the identical words used by the child which keeps the discussion centred around a child's frame of reference.

A variety of short activities are incorporated into this discussion, such as:

- On the count of three, run to that tree and come back;
- Go and find a green leaf, a red leaf and a brown leaf;
- Can anyone find a bird's feather or a very long stick?;
- Who can do ten star jumps on the spot?

This allows the session to be less intense, adds the opportunity for exercise, and allows adults the chance to check-in on how certain children are feeling.

To conclude the lesson, while the children sit under a tree eating their snack, Clare reads 'The Sad Book' by Michael Rosen which deals with loss in an inspiring and honest way.

Reflection

Consider the following questions relating to the Key Stage 1 lesson about loss.

Should I research my lesson's topic/issues?

It is crucial to research the areas you are teaching especially if you feel you lack the fundamental background knowledge. For example, Clare researched about reactions to grief in children and found that they vary according to a child's developmental stage and can be normal and/or complicated. For instance, children aged between six and nine are just able to understand the biology of death and are only just able to comprehend the finality of it. Clare also found that following a loss, many children may develop fears associated with their own death or the death of a family member. They may also develop feelings of insecurity, experience nightmares or difficulty sleeping. Some may be prone to hyperactive, aggressive and disruptive behavior, while others may be withdrawn and sad.

Is assessment worthwhile in PSHE?

Assessing a child's progress particularly in understanding their own wellbeing is important as it allows them to reflect on their individual needs and self-care. It can also increase their motivation, which establishes extra value and impact.

What is a benefit of using a picture book to end a lesson?

The PSHE Association (2019) found that pupils respond more readily when they are reflecting upon someone other than themselves, so it is effective to ask questions about how a character feels instead. The use of puppets, role-play and short film clips are also recommended. The PSHE Association (2019) stress the importance of ending the lesson in a safe and supportive way.

Key Stage 2 lesson: Mindfulness

This lesson focuses on how powerful it can be for a teacher to act as a role model when engaging in mental health strategies, such as mindfulness. It can be useful to stress to children that their mental health needs can be resolved, especially with self-care and access to help.

Seamus teaches Year 6 and has noticed that, as the SATs draw closer, many of his pupils are experiencing anxiety; many are tearful over issues that in the past he believes would not have upset them. Two parents have emailed Seamus to say that their children have been having trouble sleeping and have expressed worry about the forthcoming tests. Consequently, Seamus has decided that, in response to this need, mindfulness could be a useful exercise for his class to master. His aim is for pupils to maintain their attention and concentration on one thing at a time to allow their mind and body to have a break.

Seamus has undertaken some research and found that mindfulness can be described as 'Paying attention on purpose, non-judgementally, in the present moment' (Kabat-Zinn, 1982) or 'Consciously bringing awareness to your here-and-now experience, with openness, interest, and receptiveness' (Harris, 2007). Kabat-Zinn and Kabat-Zinn (2014) believe that mindfulness comes naturally to children as they already play in the moment. Mindfulness can teach children to support their mental health by becoming more self-aware; it can teach them compassion and to self-regulate their emotions.

Seamus incorporates the following into the school day:

- Allocating five minutes at the beginning, or end, of most lessons and merely asking his pupils to close their eyes and check in with how they are feeling both physically and mentally.
- Striking a chime bar, gong or a singing bowl to encourage children to listen and focus solely on the sound, raising their hand when they can no longer hear it.
- Listening to music together in silence.
- Focusing on the sights and smell of a candle flame flickering (adhering to the health and safety policy).
- Delivering an after-school club for those children that expressed an avid interested in mindfulness. Seamus reassures parents that there are no religious connotations attached to this club. The after-school club includes the following: body scan, safe place, walking, eating and breathing mediations. Seamus discovers that a powerful exercise includes children letting go of their worries whilst releasing balloons into the sky; they then chase the balloons, and retrieve them after they have deflated, and then repeat this with a different worry. He notices that any creative mindfulness activities tend to be well-liked – for example, painting rainbows using warm water scented with aromatherapy oils and with sequins swirling in the water pots.

Reflection

Was there any impact in Seamus including mindfulness?
Seamus noticed that children seemed calmer, more focused and motivated towards their studies and worked more collaboratively. On sharing this news with his headteacher, she introduced a positive intervention where special relaxation pods were placed outside and inside the school grounds. Pupils, and staff, could sit in these pods and meditate or listen to ocean sounds to help them escape and process their thoughts and feelings in a quiet, contemplative way. The pods gave pupils the opportunity to self-regulate their emotions and time was allocated to specific children who had high ACE (adverse childhood experiences) scores and had experienced trauma in their lives.

Points to consider and conclusion

I hope that this chapter has increased your confidence and given you a few ideas to incorporate into your teaching. It is fair to say that the recognition and supervision of the mental health and emotional wellbeing of children and school staff is bound to be particularly significant in the years following the COVID-19 crisis. This support needs to be consistent and highly prioritized in schools so that we can mitigate the detrimental effects of the pandemic, and therefore PSHE and R(S)HE's status in schools should be elevated and given the value it truly deserves within education.

Points to consider for your own setting

- Which wellbeing issues do I particularly need to address with the pupils within my setting?
- How can I encourage whole-school wellbeing in my setting?
- Would the practice of mindfulness be welcomed by the children, staff and parents of my school?
- How are strategies for school staff wellbeing modelled to our pupils?

 # Key reading

- It may be useful for you to refer to government documents, such as Transforming Children and Young People's Mental Health Provision: a Green Paper (2017) and the Government Response to the Consultation on Transforming Children and Young People's Mental Health Provision: a Green Paper and Next Steps (2018).

Further reading

- For input on mental health, I can particularly recommend the Charlie Waller Memorial Trust (https://www.cwmt.org.uk/school-training) who offer free resources and excellent speakers for a donation.
- Explore the website *Mindfulness in Schools Project* which provides useful guidance and resources. Available online: https://mindfulnessinschools.org/mindfulness-in-education/

- A teacher is not able to look after the pupils in their care unless they possess good mental health themselves. If you are interested in learning more about how to support your wellbeing as a member of school staff, please read my book: Allies, S. (2020), *Supporting Teacher Wellbeing: a practical guide for primary teachers and school leaders,* London: Routledge.
- It is crucial to highlight to staff that the Education Support Partnership (https://www.educationsupportpartnership.org.uk/) offer support and a telephone helpline which is open every day of the year: 08000 562 561.

References

Department for Education (DfE) (2018), *Mental Health and Behaviour in Schools.* Available online: https://www.gov.uk/government/publications/mental-health-and-behaviour-in-schools--2 (accessed 11 September 2019).

Department for Education (DfE) (2019), *Relationships Education, Relationships and Sex Education (RSE) and Health Education: Statutory guidance for governing bodies, proprietors, head teachers, principals, senior leadership teams and teachers.* Available online: https://www.gov.uk/government/publications/relationships-education-relationships-and-sex-education-rse-and-health-education (accessed 11 September 2019).

Education Endowment Foundation (2020), *Improving Social and Emotional Learning in Primary Schools: Six recommendations for improving social and emotional learning in primary schools.* Available online: https://educationendowmentfoundation.org.uk/public/files/Publications/SEL/EEF_SEL_Summary_of_recommendations_poster.pdf (accessed 14 May 2020).

Harris, R. (2007), *The Happiness Trap*, Boston: Robinson Press.

Kabat-Zinn, J. (1982), 'An outpatient program in behavioral medicine for chronic pain patients based on the practice of mindfulness meditation: Theoretical considerations and preliminary results.' *General Hospital Psychiatry*, 4(1), 33–47.

Kabat-Zinn, M. and Kabat-Zinn, J. (2014), *Everyday blessings: Mindfulness for parents*, United Kingdom: Piatkus.

Mental Health Foundation (2002), *A bright future for all: promoting mental health in education.* Available online: https://www.mentalhealth.org.uk/publications/bright-future-all (accessed 4 September 2019).

National Health Service (2018), *The Mental Health of Children and Young People in England.* Available online: https://digital.nhs.uk/data-and-information/publications/statistical/mental-health-of-children-and-young-people-in-england/2017/2017 (accessed 4 September 2019).

Natural England Commissioned Report (2016), *A review of nature-based interventions for mental health care.* Available online: http://publications.naturalengland.org.uk/publication/4513819616346112 (accessed 4 September 2019).

Patalay, P. and Fitzsimons, E. (2016), 'Correlates of Mental Illness and Wellbeing in Children: Are They the Same? Results from the UK Millennium Cohort Study', *Journal of the American Academy of Child and Adolescent Psychiatry,* 55 (9): 771–83.

PSHE Association (2019), *Guidance and lessons on teaching about mental health & emotional wellbeing.* Available online: https://www.pshe-association.org.uk/content/guidance-and-lessons-teaching-about-mental-health (accessed 4 September 2019).

PSHE Association (2020), *Programme of Study for PSHE Education (Key stages 1–5).* Available online: https://www.pshe-association.org.uk/curriculum-and-resources/resources/programme-study-pshe-education-key-stages-1–5 (accessed 14 May 2020).

Woolley, R. (2010), *Tackling Controversial Issues in the Primary School,* London: Routledge

13

R(S)HE: More than just the sex bit!

Victoria Pugh

This chapter will explore:

- The status of relationship and sex education in England looking at both the Relationships elements and what this means and contains as well as Sex Education;

- The ways in which consent can be discussed and taught from KS1 and how this might look within the classroom;

- How we might support pupils to understand changes to friendships and relationships.

As previously discussed in the introductory chapter, Relationships Education is to become a statutory element, along with Health Education, to be taught from September 2020. The changes signal a move towards empowering children in their understanding and exploration of healthy relationships, how to identify when a relationship is not healthy and who to go to for help if this is the case. But what does relationships education actually mean? Within the Relationships Education guidance document (DfE, 2019), Relationships Education in primary schools will cover 'Families and people who care for me', 'Caring friendships', 'Respectful relationships', 'Online relationships', and 'Being safe'. This is the first update we have seen in relationship and Sex Education since the 2000 Sex and Relationship Guidance document which is widely agreed to be long overdue. Although, in essence, relationships themselves haven't changed dramatically, the ways in which relationships are conducted and communicated have. The telephone calls to friends as teenagers in the past has been largely replaced by non-verbal forms such as Whatsapp, text messaging, Instagram stories and Facebook messenger. So, it is pleasing to see that this element of online relationships has been considered as important in the statutory guidance and a host of objectives have been designed to ensure it is being covered.

What's statutory and what's not

The nature of statutory status has been discussed previously in the Introduction; however, it is important to be 100 per cent clear on the status of what is statutory and what is not when it comes to the PSHE and R(S)HE curriculum.

For all primary schools, Relationships Education is statutory from September 2020. This means that all pupils must be taught all of the relationships education objectives by the end of KS2. It also means that due to being statutory parents *cannot* withdraw their children from this element of the curriculum. Sex Education is *not* statutory in primary schools; however, the Department for Education (DfE, 2019: 13,) 'continues to recommend . . . that all primary schools should have a sex education programme tailored to the age and the physical and emotional maturity of the pupils'. Parents can withdraw their children from sessions, which go beyond relationships education into sex education, if they feel it necessary. Schools do still have to teach the National Curriculum (NC) Science reproduction unit which contains the scientific perspectives of Sex Education and due to it being a NC requirement parents *cannot* withdraw their children from these lessons.

Health Education is statutory in all primary schools (except Independent schools which have their own mandatory health requirements to cover). Topics such as puberty have been moved to this section and parents cannot withdraw their children from these lessons.

Consent

One of the key themes running through the Relationships Education objectives (DfE, 2019) is that of permission seeking and links to safeguarding.

Objectives such as the following show clear links to consent and permission seeking:

- how to recognize if family relationships are making them feel unhappy or unsafe, and how to seek help or advice from others if needed.
- that in school and in wider society they can expect to be treated with respect by others, and that in turn they should show due respect to others, including those in positions of authority.
- the importance of permission seeking and giving in relationships with friends, peers and adults.

- what sorts of boundaries are appropriate in friendships with peers and others (including in a digital context).
- about the concept of privacy and the implications of it for both children and adults; including that it is not always right to keep secrets if they relate to being safe.
- that each person's body belongs to them, and the differences between appropriate and inappropriate or unsafe physical, and other, contact.
- how to respond safely and appropriately to adults they may encounter (in all contexts, including online) whom they do not know.
- how to recognize and report feelings of being unsafe or feeling bad about any adult.
- how to ask for advice or help for themselves or others, and to keep trying until they are heard.
- how to report concerns or abuse, and the vocabulary and confidence needed to do so.
- where to get advice, e.g. family, school and/or other sources.

Although it is expected that these objectives are met by the end of KS2, it is important that the concept of consent is introduced from an early age. The following case study is based upon a true story and looks at this concept in more depth.

Case Study 1

Julie is a PSHE coordinator and has been reviewing the new statutory guidance and objectives. She has had meetings with each of the year group teachers about the new programme of study they are implementing but one of the KS1 teachers isn't sure how to tackle the topic of consent and permission giving and is voicing concerns about the way in which she can teach it without addressing negative or distressing issues for young children. Julie herself is worried about how to tackle this in an age-appropriate way and how to lead her staff in order to reassure her about specific ways in which to teach it.

For Julie to begin to deal with this situation she needs to be clear about the school's safeguarding policy and how it links to the R(S)HE policy. There should be clear guidance within this document which should be shared with teachers so that there is a clear and shared approach to quality R(S)HE teaching.

Why is consent important?
Often when people think about consent, they immediately think about sexual consent, but consent is about more than that. From a young age our pupils need to feel in control of their bodies and their wishes heard. Situations

surrounding consent and young children can be seen during carpet time. It is not uncommon for an early years/KS1 teacher to witness pupils sitting on the carpet with another pupil playing with their hair. There are times when the pupil clearly looked uncomfortable and moves away only to find the child continuing to touch or play with their hair. In this instance it is key that pupils have the vocabulary to say, 'please stop, I don't like that' and in return to be listened to. Consent is about having the choice to say no and be listened to. Other examples of consent and permission seeking can be seen when one friend wants to hold the hand of another, and they pull away as they don't like it. Outside of school this may be when a parent/carer asks them to give person X (often a grandparent or family member) a kiss or hug when the child is clearly uncomfortable or embarrassed or simply doesn't want to. This can be a difficult concept to approach and it is not uncommon for teachers to feel the way they do in this case study, however, it is vital that these issues are addressed from a young age so that pupils know they have the right to decide who they want to show physical contact towards.

Strategies to help explore the concept of consent with KS1 children

- Teaching them to ask for permission – pupils can start to understand consent as asking for permission and not assuming that everyone wants them to hug them or kiss them and that merely asking for permission to do so gives everyone the opportunity to decide whether or not this is something they want.
- Teaching the differences between secrets and surprises. This can be an easy activity to carry out with pupils as you can use scenarios for them to discuss. It should be taught that surprises are something that makes you feel excited and happy – they should not make you feel uncomfortable, sad or worried.
- No means no. It is important that pupils understand that they can say no if they feel uncomfortable about something but likewise, they must respect it when someone else says no. For example, if someone wants play with them, they can say 'no thank you' but equally they must understand that this is reciprocal, and they must respect a friend or peer who says no thank you.
- Show pictures of designated safeguarding leads within the classroom or ask pupils who they can go to if they feel worried or need to speak to an adult.
- Teach pupils scientific names for body parts – it is important that pupils can confidently identify their body parts using scientific names. This is important to avoid confusion if a child is trying to make a disclosure.

Reflection

- How does your school approach the teaching of consent within KS1?
- What scenarios could you use in order to promote discussion or distancing activities when promoting consent.
- Do pupils in your KS1 setting know who to go to if they need help?
- At what age do you teach scientific names for body parts and is this decision clear within your R(S)HE policy?

Case Study 2

As mentioned previously R(S)HE is not just about the sex bit! Relationships education encompasses so much more. One of the key issues which teachers and practitioners will deal with on a day-to-day basis is that of friendships. These experiences can range from low level 'fall outs' to high level cases of bullying and everything in-between.

> A Year 5 child has a strong group of friends who have been close since they started school in Reception, however the teacher has noticed that one child in particularly has begun to seem isolated from the group and is very often on their own in the playground. There haven't been any obvious arguments. However, the playground supervisory staff have not always got time to feedback any incidents that happen at lunch time and generally ask the children to stop 'tattling' and sort the problems out themselves. The Year 5 teacher isn't sure what to do and decides just to keep an eye on the situation for now. Unfortunately, several weeks later the teacher finds some nasty notes in the classroom bin which are addressed to the child and realizes that the situation is somewhat more serious than first thought. The school are a values school and take part in anti-bullying week but do not follow a regular PSHE and R(S)HE programmes, as they can't seem to fit it in during the week.

This is a situation which will be familiar in some degree to the majority of teachers at some point in their career and the example encourages us to consider a range of points connected to the idea of friendships. It is not unusual for friendships to change throughout a pupil's journey through primary school and this is natural as children develop different interests, priorities, values and personality traits. However, the danger lies in the element of isolation and pupils feeling 'left out' as this can prove to be detrimental to both mental health and self-esteem. In this situation it would be pertinent for the teacher to speak to the lunch time supervisors or to establish a system by which incidents which occur on the playground can be simply documented to ensure a holistic view of pupils and their experiences throughout the day. As expressed previously the PSHE and R(S)HE policies should be accessible for *all* staff, including lunch time assistants, as they will often be in situations where safeguarding issues arise or be in a good position to observe any changes to friendships and behaviours which can then be communicated to the relevant teachers or safeguarding leads.

Often as educators and practitioners we can be guilty of being in a busy lunch time or play time situation when a child comes up to report that 'child X won't let me play' or 'they won't let me join in the game' and it is natural for the first suggestion to be that everyone has to play together. Everyone should be able to join in the game; however, this is not always the case. What about the game which is for four players only? Or the group who let a particular child play only to find that they are repeatedly cheating or spoiling the game. Is it reasonable to expect them to want to play with that child again? It is worthwhile to take a few seconds to try and assess the situation and remember that in life you might not like everyone, and this is normal! The difference is that regardless of the person being your best friend or someone who you don't enjoy spending time with they should still be treated be kindness and respect. In the case study scenario, it may be that the group are upset that the child no longer wants to play with them and have grown apart from them or it may be that they are isolating them due to a disagreement. Whatever the case it is important for pupils to know that writing notes, isolating people or negative comments online are not acceptable and can be incredibly hurtful. Instead they should be encouraged to speak to each other, calmly putting their point across and sharing how they feel if comfortable to do so. Research by Murray and Harrison (2005) highlights that whilst children's friendships can impact positively on their wellbeing, they can also be a source of stress. In the case study it is clear that the situation is no longer just a simple 'falling out' which is resolved quickly but has been going on for a longer period of time which would indicate that the parties involved may need help or guidance in dealing with the problem. Whilst Wooley (2010 cited in Mason and Wooley, 2019: 106) argues that:

> fairness is an effective concept to use when helping children to develop respect, by asking a child whether they felt their actions or words were fair to another child. Using questions can help children to think through the consequence of their words and actions and to begin to internalize an understanding of how to behave towards others in a range of situations

One whole-school strategy which can be particularly effective is to replace anti-bullying week with random acts of kindness and respect week. If there is a quality PSHE and R(S)HE programme in place pupils have a clearer understanding of what is kind and unkind, what healthy friendships looks like and how to deal with common fall outs. The week instead can be dedicated to ways in which they can develop their understanding of what they value in a friend and how they can be a better friend. This positive approach addresses the ways in which pupils can develop friendship rather stories around bullying which can be very negative. However, if bullying has been reported or identified it is important that it is listened to and taken seriously. The Anti-Bullying Alliance (2017) recommends ten principles to prevent and respond to bullying, which include celebrating difference, understanding and challenging vocabulary, a link to which can be found in the Further reading section at the end of the chapter.

This situation may also link to general puberty changes which may be impacting upon the pupils at this age. A programme of lessons which link to Puberty and the statutory Health Education objectives can be a useful tool in which to discuss the fact that puberty is not just about physical changes but also changes in mood, patience and levels of independence. Lessons such as these can help to allow pupils to explore the emotions and feelings which have already arisen or might arise due to hormones or changing situations. One practical way in which to explore puberty and the changes which arise is to create some 'puberty bags'.

These are gift bags which can contain items such as:

- Deodorant
- Toothpaste
- Sanitary towels
- Tampons
- Alternative menstruation products such as menstrual cups or period pants
- Tissues
- Razor (in sealed packs obviously!)
- Body wash
- Hot water bottle
- Trainers (or pictures of sportswear)
- A range of cut-out emojis.

Encouraging pupils to look at each item and decide how it might be connected to puberty. Some discussion will centre around issues: to symbolize increased emotions; trainers which link to the importance of moving and exercise on good mental health and healthy lives; and emojis to symbolize the range of emotions we can feel throughout the day. The emojis can be used to increase emotional literacy to give pupils the vocabulary to express their feelings and emotions. These discussions can then be developed further to think about the ways in which we change growing up and how friendships might be one of those changes. In the example from the case study, lessons focusing on the follow objectives from the Relationships section would be useful:

- how important friendships are in making us feel happy and secure, and how people choose and make friends.
- the characteristics of friendships, including mutual respect, truthfulness, trustworthiness, loyalty, kindness, generosity, trust, sharing interests and experiences and support with problems and difficulties.
- that healthy friendships are positive and welcoming towards others, and do not make others feel lonely or excluded.
- that most friendships have ups and downs, and that these can often be worked through so that the friendship is repaired or even strengthened, and that resorting to violence is never right.

Another strategy which can be used to explore issues which arise in the class using distancing techniques is that of scenarios. This allows issues to be discussed and debated without mentioning real names or focusing on a personal incident. It also allows for pupils to speak freely about the ways in which they might deal with a similar situation and independently reflect upon their own choices. Not only do scenarios draw attention to particular behaviours, events and reactions but they also encourage a solution-focused style approaches. Using scenarios to explore what a healthy friendship looks like, and identifying unhealthy friendship traits such as manipulation, not sharing in the other child's joy, lying about them and monopolizing the friendship. In the example case study, it is imperative that the Year 5 teacher talks to the child who is being left out, identifies the problems were possible and ensure that a strong programme which meets the relationships objectives are part of the curriculum. It is likely that the child's parents and carers will need to be informed and although this can be a difficult conversation to address it is necessary in this case.

Reflection

- As a school how do you deal with bullying and incidents involving friendship fall outs?
- Do the procedures in place allow time for clear communication between lunch time staff and teachers in order to give a full picture of the pupils' day?
- Have the break time and lunch time staff received training on mediation or conflict resolution? If not, how might you facilitate this?
- Is there opportunity for peer mediation to occur and how might training for this be facilitated and led?
- How can you develop the idea of what makes a healthy friendship whilst also acknowledging that sometimes even the best of friends disagrees or have arguments?
- When does a healthy relationship become unhealthy?

Points to consider and conclusion

R(S)HE is about so much more than 'just the sex bit'. Lessons which provide a range of discussions around healthy friendships, consent, changes in relationships and where to go for help are a welcome addition to the statutory curriculum as they will allow pupils to explore issues which they experience in their own friendships in a safe and supportive environment, whilst giving them the power to say no when they feel uncomfortable. A spiral curriculum can be powerful when encouraging pupils to develop skills and content knowledge for topics such as friendships and consent as their understanding can be built upon and developed year upon year and then applied in a range of contexts. Teaching conflict resolution skills, managing anger and how to communicate feelings effectively and calmly are key skills which need to be considered in both KS1 and KS2 in order for pupils to be able to independently deal with situations which might arise in their own friendships. With lessons which support the promotion of healthy friendships, dealing with differences and communicating effectively, we can give pupils the tools they need to form and maintain meaningful and healthy friendships based upon mutual respect, kindness and support.

Points to consider for your setting

- At what point within a friendship fall-out situation do you involve parents?
- How does your curriculum encourage pupils to explore the concept of consent and how to speak up when they feel uncomfortable in situations where they feel their voice is not being heard?
- What strategies are pupils being taught to deal with conflict, arguments or disagreements?
- How is consent taught as part of a spiral curriculum within your school and how is this evidenced?
- How can you promote and teach Emotional Literacy within the classroom or school effectively?

Key reading

- Binfet, J. (2015), 'Not-so Random Acts of Kindness: A Guide to Intentional Kindness in the Classroom', *International Journal of Emotional Education*, 7 (2): 49–62.
- Mason, S. and Woolley, R. (2019), *Relationships and sex education 3-11: supporting children's development and well-being*, 2nd edn. London: Bloomsbury Academic.

Further reading

- Anti-Bullying Alliance (2017), *10 Key principles.* Available online: https://www. anti-bullyingalliance.org.uk/tools-information/all-about-bullying/preventing-bullying-and-ethos/10-key-principles (accessed 21 September 2019).
- NSPCC (2018), *PANTS – Resources for Schools and Teachers.* Available online: www.nspcc.org.uk/preventingabuse/keeping-children-safe/underwear-rule/underwear-rule-schools-teaching-resources (accessed 21 September 2019).
- Schonert-Reichl, K. A., Schonert-Reichl, K .A., Smith, V., Smith, V., Zaidman-Zait, A., Zaidman-Zait, A., Hertzman, C. and Hertzman, C. (2012). 'Promoting Children's Prosocial Behaviors in School: Impact of the 'Roots of Empathy' Program on the Social and Emotional Competence of School-Aged Children', *School Mental Health*, 4 (1): 1–21.

References

Anti-Bullying Alliance (2017), *10 Key principles.* Available online: https://www.anti-bullyingalliance.org.uk/tools-information/all-about-bullying/preventing-bullying-and-ethos/10-key-principles (accessed 21 September 2019).

Department for Education (DfE) (2019), *Relationships Education, Relationships and Sex Education (RSE) and Health Education: statutory guidance for governing bodies, proprietors, head teachers, principals, senior leadership teams, teachers.* Available online: https://www.pshe-association.org.uk/curriculum-and-resources/resources/programme-study-pshe-education-key-stages-1%E2%80%935 (accessed 21 September 2019).

Mason, S. and Woolley, R. (2019), *Relationships and sex education 3–11: supporting children's development and well-being.* 2nd edn. London: Bloomsbury Academic.

Murray, E., and Harrison, L. J. (2005), 'Children's Perspectives on their First Year of School: Introducing a New Pictorial Measure of School Stress', *European Early Childhood Education Research Journal,* 13 (1): 111–27.

14

Resilience in an Online World

Dr Jenny Hatley and Victoria Pugh

This chapter explores:

- Ways in which schools can work with parents to highlight the importance of partnerships in building children's resilience online;

- The importance of 'managed risk' for pupils in a move towards critical thinking and self-regulation skills;

- Ways in which we can highlight the need to be critical online and to question what we see and read.

The pace of change with technology is huge. Things develop at a rapid rate and it is often difficult for parents and teachers to keep up with young people's experiences online. More children are engaging with digital media than ever before and whilst this brings many benefits, it also brings challenges and risks. For example, underage use of social media platforms, online gaming, pornography and sexting are all areas of concern. Whilst exposure to online risks does not necessarily cause harm, as professionals who work with children we do want to help our young people manage these risks well.

This chapter explores two case studies, one for each of KS1 and KS2. Whilst they are fictional, they represent an amalgamation of children's experiences that they have brought to the authors during their years teaching in the classroom.

Case Study 1: Key Stage 1

This case study shows the link between experiences, emotions and behaviour.

A child comes into the classroom tearful and tired, which seems out of character for this usually buoyant member of the class. Rather than heading straight for the play corner as they usually would, they go to the book corner and immediately start annoying the other children there. Very soon after this, the teaching assistant intervenes. The child is given a warning, however after repeated similar episodes throughout the morning, they find themselves moved down the zone board. The teacher takes some time to talk to them and quickly discovers that the child is tired due to playing on their brother's tablet after bedtime without their carer's knowledge. Furthermore, the teacher discovers that the child had been playing online games which were not appropriate for their age and had heard lots of bad language and things they did not understand from older children.

There is a reason behind the child's emotional reactions. They are secondary emotions coming from tiredness. The child is also experiencing anxiousness and confusion from content that they did not understand since it was not appropriate for their age. They also experienced guilt because they did not have permission from their brother or their carer to use the tablet and they knew it was wrong to watch it after bedtime. The knock-on effects of the intervention from the TA in the class, who in this instance had not understood the link between emotions and behaviour, meant that the child was punished which further compounded their negative experience. The teacher did have this understanding, and their intervention to explore the reasons for the child's behaviour enabled them to understand the child and help them to manage their experience. It would also have enabled them to highlight any safeguarding issues that may have been present, potentially missed with a focus purely on the child's external behaviour.

According to a report by Ofcom (2017), 42 per cent of KS1 pupils have their own tablets whilst 82 per cent of KS1 pupils are online for almost ine hours a week. Studies by Marinelli et al. (2014) also highlighted the key links between screen time and shorted or disturbed sleep experienced by children with possible causes being over-stimulation from content and the effects of light emissions on melatonin levels. It is essential that pupils have an understanding of the effects of excess or prolonged screen time on sleep and wellbeing.

Forming strong parent partnerships are essential in order need to encourage parents to see their children's online safety and wellbeing primarily as their responsibility and not something that is only done by the school. Pointing them towards parental controls is one thing which can be helpful, but many children can bypass these, often without their parent's knowledge.

Parents need to educate themselves and there are many sources of support for this.

As a school this partnership between home and school could come in the form of:

- Newsletters with links to parent's information sites and educational resources on ways to ensure safe screen time and social media use for children.
- Holding training sessions which help to inform parents on how to help their children to recognize when they have had enough screen time or how to limit their screen time and information on the ways in which the overuse or incorrect use of social media and screen time can affect behaviour and mood.
- Research homework projects for pupils which ask them to work with their parents to find out about the effects of screen time and social media use on their behaviour, mental health and sleep and the recommendations provided for this.
- Websites such as 'Digital parenting' by Vodaphone, 'National Online Safety' and 'UK Safer Internet Online' are particularly useful for parents and make for good recommendations or links to share.

In addition, raising awareness about online gaming can also be helpful. Whilst the game itself might be age-appropriate, what happens within the game might be an area of concern. For example, through connecting online with other children they may be playing with much older young people who are not as respectful in their use of language or behaviour as we encourage our children to be. This may expose our children to difficulty, as shown in the example above. Within school we can teach about PEGI age-rating labels and what these mean, however there must be parental support for pupils in order for the child to be able to make healthy and informed choices about the games they play and content they view.

Total restriction of the use of technology is not helpful either for parents or school as the benefits of technology provide pupils with creative outlets for their learning, opportunities to engage with the wider world and a wealth of information which is available instantly. However, due to risks associated with technology, a common reaction is to stop the child from using it, but this is not the answer. Whilst the primary responsibility lies with the parents and strong partnerships are needed in this area, even more important is developing the child's self-regulation skills and resilience in order for them to deal with any situation themselves, whether or not an adult is around. Digital access is so mobile, it is unreasonable to think that an adult can be with them at all times when using their devices and, as stated, parental controls are not always enough. Children need to develop the ability to self-regulate behaviour and emotion; even within KS1 they can do so.

Managed exposure to online risk is important. On the basis that a good PSHE classroom already supports positive relationships and the setting of ground rules, a key aspect of building resilience online with young children is providing opportunities within the classroom for them to experience risk in a managed environment where, as a first step, the teacher is available to talk with children about what they are feeling when they experience the risk, but quickly moves the child on to understanding how they can manage their own feelings in response to the teacher's advice, applying this then to future risk experiences. It is necessary to understand that exposure to risk online does not necessarily cause harm (Livingstone and O'Neill, 2014). A factor that helps to reduce potential harm is the building of resilience which occurs from managed exposure to previous risks.

Building a critical attitude is vital. Alongside the fostering of resilience, the building of a questioning attitude towards online content (termed 'criticality') is an essential skill. Children need to develop this in order to be able to judge the level of risk inherent in different types of content and therefore make healthy choices about what they consume online, regardless of any adult presence. There are some important principles in developing criticality. These principles include:

- Ensuring that supportive relationships between the teacher and children exist and are nurtured.
- Not getting 'told off' if they've looked at something they shouldn't have, but rather have supportive conversations to identify correct choices.
- Ongoing attention to good emotional literacy as a general feature of school life.
- Planning opportunities for exposure to *managed* risk. For example, create deliberate untruths on the school website for children to spot. Children could ask: Is this real? Is it true? How do I know? If I am unsure who could I ask? How do I know this person is the right person to ask? What can I do if I find out the information is fake? Does what I have seen online give me an uncomfortable feeling? What can I do about this? These question prompts could be used to get children to engage with the information and reflect on their own response, rather than being told to automatically ask an adult. This way, they develop independence, criticality and resilience when dealing with online content.
- Looking at a range of 'news' and working out whether is it real or fake and how we know.

Through a series of well-structured lessons which directly teach these digital literacy skills pupils are empowered to be part of their own decision-making when it comes to technology and to ensure that they understand this in relation to their own wellbeing.

Reflection

- What opportunities for managed risk do your pupils have within their school day?
- How strong is your school/parent/carer partnership and are you providing opportunities to help parents/carers develop their understanding of digital literacy?
- Where in your PSHE curriculum is there an opportunity for pupils to develop their understanding of the importance of sleep and the ways in which to manage their own time online or on devices?

Case Study 2: Key Stage 2

The Children's Commissioner's report on the effects of social media use on eight to twelve year olds, *Life in 'Likes'* (Children's Commissioner, 2018), quotes research showing that 75 per cent of ten to twelve year olds have a social media account, despite the official age limit of thirteen years. Whilst this chapter focuses on KS2, it is important to highlight from the report that many Year 7 pupils find social media hard to manage, that they are becoming dependent on likes and comments for social validation and that they are also changing their behaviour offline to fit an online image, leading to increased anxiety as they try to keep up appearances as they get older (Children's Commissioner, 2018). Whilst it is important not to minimize the benefits of social media use, such as increased connections and access to excellent content, it is necessary to consider how we can help our KS2 children manage their social media use such that they can be resilient in the face of social media pressures. After all, it won't be long before our KS2 children are in Year 7. In doing so, we acknowledge the official position that they should not have accounts on social media, but at the same time wish to support teachers and other adults dealing with the reality that many do.

A child comes into the class and is reluctant to sit in their seat, spending more time than usual by their drawer. Whilst it is school policy that children must lock their mobile phones in the school office on their way into school, the teacher notices that they are still playing with their phone and when they tell the child to bring the phone to them, the child becomes angry and anxious and continues using their phone. The teacher walks over and demands that the phone is handed over and that the child joins the class. As the child gives the teacher their phone, several notifications appear on the screen from several social media platforms. Since the screen shows previews of the messages, the teacher notices that whilst some are harmless, some are commenting on the child's looks in response to photos the child has posted. The teacher then realizes that the child has changed their hair recently and is wearing their uniform in a more mature way. The teacher is concerned that the child's social media use has become inappropriate and seems to be having an adverse effect.

Once again, the link here between emotions and behaviour is clear. At issue too, is the relationship between online and offline worlds. Whilst young people have grown up with technology and therefore do not see the distinction between the two worlds, as adults this is often not the case. What happens online can have a large effect on young people's offline behaviour, and vice versa.

In light of the blurred boundary between online and offline worlds, 'friendships' shown in likes and comments on social media posts can feel as real as offline friendships. The emotions in response to online behaviour are also just as real. Even though technology has advanced, our emotional and relational skills in response to it have not. It is important not to minimize pupil's experiences of online friendships as 'not real' or 'just virtual' and to bring them into discussion with children when having any other discussions about, for example, what makes a good friendship. There are specific issues related to social media however – such as the fact that many posts are exaggerated. Someone can promote an online appearance that isn't real, leading to others feeling envy or, as stated in the *Life in 'Likes' report*, anxious and needing to keep up appearances. Highlighting this to children such that they begin to see that they may be aspiring to an ideal which is unattainable can help to bring their experiences back down to earth and also help them to judge what they are seeing more critically.

The relationship between body image and social media has been highly documented with researchers such as Grogan (2016) and Kerner et al.,(2018) suggesting that social media sites such as Facebook combine peer pressure and media influence which have been shown to have negative effects on individuals perceptions of their own body image. A report by The Children's Commissioner, *Life in 'Likes'* (2018) found that 'Older girls (10 – 12) worried about being "pretty", with a particular focus on having clear skin and nice hair, but with little mention of how their bodies looked. This could possibly be due to the fact that most of the photos they shared of themselves on Instagram and Snapchat (and saw of other people) were selfies from the shoulders up.' There is also evidence that body dissatisfaction develops during childhood with 40 to 50 per cent of six to twelve year olds reporting that they are unhappy with the way they look (Smolak, 2011). It would seem therefore that early intervention and education is vital to ensure that our pupils gain the knowledge and understanding that not everything they see online is real. It can also be helpful to show pupils pictures of photos which are online pre and post Photoshop to highlight the ways in which images can be altered with discussions around why they are altered and debating if they feel this is right or not. Organizations such as Media Smart offer free resources aimed at nine to eleven year olds which explore the use of advertising and its influence on body image. These can be used as springboards for discussion or to share with parents to ensure that they are aware of social media filters, Photoshopping and fake photos. Workshops where pupils, parents and teachers work together can be a valuable way to create fake photos, experiment with Photoshop and filters in order to experience the ways in which photos and images can be altered and the importance of being critical when viewing them online.

Ensuring that your curriculum provides lessons on trolling and negative social media comments and how to deal with them is essential. Some key ways in which to explore these issues with KS2 can be through the use of distancing techniques such as:

- Scenarios
- Problem page answers
- Graffiti walls
- Question boxes
- Hot seat interviews
- Creating how-to-guides for younger children.

All of these techniques allow for pupils to experience examples of trolling or negative social media comments in a safe environment without being directly involved. It helps to create an experience which they can assess and develop a strategy to respond to so that if they are ever in a similar situation, they have the skills to deal with it independently if necessary. It is also important to consider why people might post negative or unkind comments online and explore the range of emotions or reasons which might prompt such actions.

Some of the considerations of the KS1 case study are also relevant here. Restricting the use of social media is unlikely to work and certainly being risk-averse in our approach can be counterproductive leaving pupils with limited or no experiences to draw upon. As stated, exposure to managed risk in a supported environment can help build resilience and can develop criticality. Teaching these management skills, for example knowing when to recognize something as 'fake' and how and when to seek support, plus the ongoing support of good emotional literacy and the building of self-esteem as part of school culture, can help children to self-regulate and be resilient in the face of pressures from not just social media but when using other digital media as well.

Reflection

- Do the images on your presentations and around the school show diversity and 'real life' people?
- What advice do you share with pupils on strategies for identifying fake news, Photoshopping and trolling?
- How can you promote positive body image from a young age?

Points to consider and conclusion

This chapter has highlighted several key principles which can help pupils in KS1 and KS2 manage their online experiences. Technology will continue to advance, and it is unrealistic to expect ourselves as teachers or parents to keep up with all that young people are doing online and therefore need to arm pupils with the tools to address these issues when/if they experience them. Body image campaigns and self-esteem workshops can be useful in highlighting the importance of individuality and being happy 'in your own skin'. However, this needs to be an ethos which runs throughout all lessons, subjects and day-to-day interactions with pupils in order to really build a strong message. In supporting children to be able to self-regulate and manage their own online lives, we can help them to keep themselves safe, healthy and happy.

Points to consider for your setting

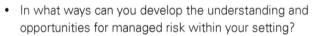

- In what ways can you develop the understanding and opportunities for managed risk within your setting?
- How might you support parents/carers to support their children online?
- What is your general approach to social media as a school in terms of pupil access? We know that the minimum age restrictions for Facebook is thirteen years old but what happens if pupils are experiencing issues with other pupils from school on social media platforms such as this. Is it a school issue or one to be dealt with by parents? How would your school or setting respond?

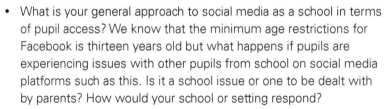

Key reading

- Children's Commissioner (2018), *Life in 'likes' report*. Available online: https://www.childrenscommissioner.gov.uk/wp-content/uploads/2018/01/Childrens-Co mmissioner-for-England-Life-in-Likes.pdf (accessed on 27 September 2019).
- Livingstone, S. and O'Neill, B. (2014), 'Children's rights online: challenges, dilemmas and emerging directions', in van der Hof, S., van den Berg, B., and Schermer, B. (eds), *Minding Minors Wandering the Web: Regulating Online Child Safety,* 19–38, Berlin: Springer.
- UK Council for Child Internet Safety (2018), *Education for a Connected World*. Available online: https://www.gov.uk/government/publications/education-for-a-connected-world (accessed on 27 September 2019).

Further reading

- Childnet (2017), *Social Media Guide Teachers and Support Staff*. Available online: https://www.childnet.com/ufiles/Social-Media-Guide-teachers-and-professionals.pdf (accessed 27 September 2019).
- Hale, L. and Guan, S. (2015), 'Screen time and sleep among school-aged children and adolescents: A systematic literature review', *Sleep Medicine Reviews*, 21: 50–8.
- Hutchinson, N. and Calland, C. (2011), *Body image in the primary school*, London: Routledge.

References

Children's Commissioner (2018), *Life in 'likes' report*. Available online: https://www.childrenscommissioner.gov.uk/wp-content/uploads/2018/01/Childrens-Co mmissioner-for-England-Life-in-Likes.pdf (accessed 27 September 2019).

Grogan, S. (2016), *Body image: understanding body dissatisfaction in men, women and children*, 3rd edn, London: Routledge.

Kerner, C., Haerens, L. and Kirk, D. (2018), 'Understanding body image in physical education: Current knowledge and future directions', *European Physical Education Review*, 24 (2): 255–65.

Livingstone, S. and O'Neill, B. (2014), 'Children's rights online: challenges, dilemmas and emerging directions', in van der Hof, S., van den Berg, B., and Schermer, B. (eds), *Minding Minors Wandering the Web: Regulating Online Child Safety*, 19–38, Berlin: Springer.

Marinelli, M., Sunyer, J., Alvarez-Pedrerol, M., Iñiguez, C., Torrent, M., Vioque, J., Turner, M. C. and Julvez, J. (2014), 'Hours of television viewing and sleep duration in children: A multicenter birth cohort study', *JAMA Pediatrics*, 168 (5): 458–64.

Ofcom (2017), *Children and parents: Media use and attitudes report*. Available online: https://www.ofcom.org.uk/research-and-data/media-literacy-research/childrens/children-parents-2017 (accessed 27 September 2019).

Smolak, L. (2011), 'Body image development in childhood', in T. F. Cash and L. Smolak, eds, *Body Image: A handbook of science, practice and prevention*, 67–75, London: Guilford Press.

15

R(S)HE and Faith Schools

Richard Woolley

This chapter explores:

- Ways in which primary schools with a religious character may approach Relationships Education;

- The views of a range of religious and non-religious people;

- How by engaging in genuine dialogue resolution can be found when differences exist.

Faith and belief can be intensely personal parts of a person's being. They inform how individuals see the world, how they view its workings, how they understand how that world came into being and the values they apply when interacting with others. Such an approach may involve a belief in a supernatural being or beings (referred to as God or gods), an appreciation of the workings of nature, creation and/or evolution, rational and scientific interpretations of the world, or a mixture from these. How a person interacts with the world around them, and appreciates their place within it, are affected by their faith and belief (including those with no faith or any adherence to a particularly religious viewpoint).

Religion and context

Despite falling numbers, Christianity remained the largest religion in England and Wales at the time of the last census in 2011 (33.2 million people). Muslims were the next biggest religious group (2.7 million people) and had grown by 1.8 per cent to 4.8 per cent of the population over the previous decade. Notably, the proportion who reported they had no religion reached a quarter of the population (14.1 million people) (ONS, undated). The religion question was the only voluntary question on the 2011 census and 7.2 per cent of people did not answer. Between 2001 and 2011 there had been a decrease in people who identify as Christian (from 71.7 per cent to 59.3 per cent) and an increase in those reporting no religion (from 14.8 per cent to 25.1 per cent). This means that those reporting no religion or declining to answer totalled 32.3 per cent of the population (ONS, undated). This provides some context to the environment in which the school system operates.

As well as considering the religious make-up of the population, it is essential to reflect on what is meant by the term faith school. According to the UK government:

- Faith schools have to teach the National Curriculum but can choose what they teach in religious studies.
- They may have different staffing policies or admissions criteria to other schools, although anyone can apply for a place.
- Faith academies do not have to teach the National Curriculum and have their own admissions processes (Gov.uk, no date).

In England the school system is made up of a diverse range of schools funded by the state, some of which are provided by religious organizations and state-aided or controlled. The Church of England is the largest provider of schools with a religious character:

- Around one-third of the 24,000 schools in England are faith schools, with over two-thirds of these being affiliated to the Church of England, and almost one-third Roman Catholic.
- Approximately 1 million children attend Church of England schools.
- About 15 million people alive today went to a Church of England school.
- A quarter of primary schools and over 200 secondary schools are Church of England.
- With 250 sponsored and over 650 converter academies, the Church is the biggest sponsor of academies in England (Church of England, undated).

Interestingly, statutory guidance on Relationships Education (DfE, 2019) applies to all state funded schools including free schools and academies.

Equality and diversity

It is important to note that within religious faiths there exists a plurality of viewpoints relating to sex and relationships. There are diverse views on matters such as contraception, divorce, same-sex partnerships and cohabitation. What is acceptable to one believer may be an anathema to others within their religion, particularly those with a more fundamentalist or conservative outlook. Whilst some believers argue that more progressive – and inclusive – approaches to relationships and sex education go against traditional teachings rooted in religious scriptures, others believe that traditions and holy writings need to be interpreted and reinterpreted in the light of the evolving social world in which we live.

It is also important to remind ourselves that the Equality Act (2010) introduced nine protected characteristics, drawing together a range of legislation developed in preceding decades:

- Age
- Disability
- Gender Reassignment
- Marriage and Civil Partnership
- Pregnancy and maternity
- 'Race' (this includes ethnic or national origins, or nationality)
- Religion or belief
- Sex
- Sexual orientation.

A key provision in the Act is the Public Sector Equality Duty, which places a general duty on public authorities, including schools, to be proactive in addressing inequalities. The law protects individuals from discrimination whether direct or indirect, by association or perception. It is notable that the protection for religion and belief includes discrimination by people of the same religion, it also protects those of no religion.

Inevitably, people with strongly held and fervent views will disagree. Under the Equality Act (2010) these people have a right to be respected and not to be discriminated against as a result of a protected characteristic. Thus, a committed religious person may fervently believe that it is not acceptable to live in a same-sex relationship, whilst a gay person may be happily married. Of course, other religious people may support equal marriage, and other gay people may feel that marriage is an outdated institution and inappropriate in the modern day. Views are diverse and sometimes polarized. Finding a way for such diverse individuals to reach agreement is not only difficult, it is probably impossible. That said, each is entitled to their view and with that right comes the responsibility to respect the views of others.

Case Study 1: Key Stage 1

It is important to remember that practice has not always been as inclusive as it is in some schools in the present day. The following example predates the Equality Act (2010) by a couple of years, but still serves as a stark example of how a teacher's personal views can be inappropriately expressed in a professional context:

> A former colleague recounted to me the story of a child in Year 1 who drew his family during a lesson focussing on 'Our Homes':
>
>> He drew his mum, with whom he lived, and his two dads; mum and dad had separated not long after he was born, and dad now lived with his male partner. His teacher asked who the second man was, and when told responded: 'We don't want to see that here.' She told the child to rub out his father's partner.
>>
>> Woolley, 2008: 115

The Local Government Act of 1988 had forbidden the intentional promotion of homosexuality or the publication of materials to promote homosexuality. Section 28 of the Act stated that a Local Authority should not 'promote the teaching in any maintained school of the acceptability of homosexuality as a pretended family relationship' (Legislation.gov.uk, undated). Although repealed in 2003, as recently as 2013 it was identified that anti-bullying policies in some schools in England still reflected the earlier legislation (Morris, 2013). Although technically the Local Government Act (1988) did not apply to schools, teachers were left feeling vulnerable, unsure of their own position in relation to the Act and cautious about speaking about LGBT+ relationships with their pupils. Later, guidance indicated that no particular sexual orientation should be promoted as this would be 'inappropriate teaching' (DfEE, 2000: 5).

Only with the publication of new statutory guidance on Relationships Education (2019) has an overt reference to diverse ways of being family been included in the school curriculum. Remarkably the previous guidance published in 2000 remained in place for two decades, written at a time when Section 28 was still in law and the Equality Act a decade away. The 2019 document is effective from September 2020, with all primary schools required to deliver Relationships Education (and able to choose whether to deliver Sex Education). There is no right for parents and carers to ask that their child be excused from Relationships Education.

Human dignity and shared humanity

In the introduction to the second edition of *Valuing All God's Children*, Most Reverend and Right Honourable Justin Welby, Archbishop of Canterbury, states:

> Central to Christian theology is the truth that every single one of us is made in the image of God. Every one of us is loved unconditionally by God. We must avoid, at all costs, diminishing the dignity of any individual

to a stereotype or a problem. Church of England schools offer a community where everyone is a person known and loved by God, supported to know their intrinsic value

Church of England, 2017: 1

This view of the all-encompassing love of God will not sit comfortably with those who do not accept such a faith-based interpretation of the world. However, the sentiments of human dignity and the sense of a shared common humanity will be recognizable to most, if not all, people. The Church of England takes the view that the dehumanizing impact of bullying must be challenged in order to establish safe and secure learning environments where all can flourish:

> No school can claim to be a safe, loving and protective institution whilst members of the school community are suffering and being made unhappy through bullying. Leaders in Church of England schools need to be committed to ensuring they build a school culture and community where all staff members and pupils feel confident and supported in challenging homophobic, biphobic and transphobic bullying.

Church of England, 2017: 9

In order to address such bullying, children need to be aware of what is and is not acceptable in terms of language and behaviours. This necessitates acknowledging, valuing and celebrating difference. In particular, *Valuing All God's Children* addresses issues that it is anticipated will be faced in primary schools.

This stands in contrast to the example from practice identified in the opening to this case study, where a child's home circumstances are unvalued by a member of the teaching profession. Feeling accepted, welcomed and valued is an essential part of the environment required in order for learning to take place, and one might argue that whilst every school should have such values at the heart of their ethos this should be especially true for faith schools, as is reflected by the words of the Archbishop of Canterbury above.

This case study addresses the need, identified in the Statutory Guidance for RSE (DfE, 2019) for pupils to know by the end of primary school:

> that others' families, either in school or in the wider world, sometimes look different from their family, but that they should respect those differences and know that other children's families are also characterised by love and care.

DfE, 2019: 20

and

> the importance of respecting others, even when they are very different from them (for example, physically, in character, personality or backgrounds), or make different choices or have different preferences or beliefs.

DfE, 2019: 21

Reflection

Reflecting on the issues raised in Case Study 1, consider:

- How you would react to a teacher behaving in the way outlined in the opening section.
- Whether you feel it is possible to 'promote' any kind of sexual orientation or sexuality.
- Whether the views and values expressed in the excerpts from *Valuing All God's Children* are distinctive to Christianity or held more widely.

Case Study 2: Key Stage 2

Salma has been exploring the topic of weddings from different religions with her Year 4 class. Over a series of lessons, the children have looked at different rites and traditions within major world faiths, with some bringing photographs and artefacts from home to show how marriage is celebrated in their own culture.

Harminder brought in the invitation to his mums' wedding, which was being planned for later in the year. Everyone in the class was aware that Harminder had two mums, but some children were surprised that they were going to get married. Salma decided that it was appropriate to use this opportunity to talk about marriage within the broad legal context of the United Kingdom using time allocated for Relationships Education. This provided a catalyst to focus on the relationships aspect of the children's learning and reflections, rather than the processes, symbols and practices associated with the discussion in the RE lessons.

Using *Donovan's Big Day* by Lesléa Newman (2011) Salma structured discussion around Donovan's feelings on his big day, the preparations he makes, how he is supported by members of his wider family, and the role he plays as ring-bearer for Mommy and Mama. The book provided a distancing technique to discuss Donovan's experience, without focusing on Harminder and his situation. Salma reflected:

I hadn't realised how much the learning about weddings had focused on what people wore, what they ate, the words used during the ceremonies and the role of families and friends. I had been so focused on the practical and religious elements of the subject, that I had really missed the whole point: that the wedding was about two people expressing their love and commitment for each other. By seeking to make links with Harminder's experience, we found an additional dimension that I need to make sure I keep when I repeat this topic again in future years. It seems pretty obvious to me now, and there is an irony that this essential element of the topic could easily have been missed.

It is interesting to consider whether Salma's approach to teaching about marriage is different because she works in a school with a religious character. As a Church of England school aided by the state, the school is able to set its own admissions policy and designs its own curriculum for the teaching or Religious Education. The school is based in an area with significant religious and ethnic diversity. Many of the parents choose the school because of its open approach to discussing matters relating to faith, and its ethos that makes clear that a faith commitment is an important part of everyday life. Fundamental to the school's ethos is its commitment to celebrating difference and diversity; affirming that everyone is different and special.

This raises an interesting aspect of the debate around how diverse views are able to live alongside one another. The school affirms the importance of valuing faith and respecting those who do not have a particular religious faith. This is very much in the spirit of the Equality Act (2010). However, celebrating difference is significantly different to tolerating difference (Halstead and Reiss, 2003: 103). The word tolerance can feel begrudging, one tolerates someone or something, and we suggest that respect is a more positive and affirming term. However, learning to respect someone who holds a view we believe to be wrong or against all that we believe to be good and true is not easy. This is the situation that some people with religious belief find themselves in: they see the world in a particular way, with values that they believe are set out by God and therefore immutable.

Herein lies the nub of the issue. The challenges are not about faith schools and non-faith schools and whether/how their ethos or focus might be different. Rather, the complexity comes when people with one particular and heartfelt view come into contact with other who have equally genuine and heartfelt views, and the two differ. Such views may be about the use of contraception, whether divorce is valid and on what grounds, or approaches to LGBT+ relationships. It is more appropriate to talk about people who, for example, support same-sex marriage and those who don't than to infer that there is a particular religious standpoint on the issue. Clearly people of faith differ in their views and what they feel is acceptable or not acceptable. Focusing on the topic where the disagreement arises, and not on the person's justification for that disagreement, will help avoid stereotyping people of faith as for or against whatever issue is causing debate. Of course, that does not help to find a resolution, but it does stop misrepresenting religious groups and it reminds us that no religion consists of people with a single homogenous view. Of course, some people will disagree with this approach, and whilst we appreciate their difference, we also know that we have the rights and responsibilities to express our own view in our quest to promote inclusion and celebrate difference.

This case study addresses the need, identified in the Statutory Guidance for RSE (DfE, 2019) for pupils to know by the end of primary school:

that families are important for children growing up because they can give love, security and stability.

DfE, 2019: 20

that marriage represents a formal and legally recognised commitment of two people to each other which is intended to be lifelong.

DfE, 2019: 21

Reflection

Reflecting on the issues raised in Case Study 2, consider:

- How you might respond to a parent or carer who feels it inappropriate to speak about Harminder's family with the class.
- Whether you agree with the idea that there is a potential tension between 'tolerating' and 'celebrating' someone's beliefs or way of life.
- How a teacher might create the context to discuss diverse forms of marriage with a class of children where such diversity was not apparent.

Further picturebooks showing a diversity of ways of being family are included in the *Family Diversities Reading Resource* an online annotated bibliography freely available to schools and other education settings. A link is included in the Key reading section at the end of this chapter.

Points to consider and conclusion

This chapter has explored issues which some readers will find uncomfortable or contentious. We are all different and hold a variety of views about both religious faith and relationships education, as well as how the two may interact. Our beliefs can be personal and passionately held, and this can make sharing them and discussing them with those who hold differing views difficult. It is important that we do not avoid such dialogue, and that we engage in it in a respectful and caring manner.

We have noted that a significant number of schools in England are of a religious character, but this does not mean that the children, parents/carers, staff or governors all share the same viewpoints. We also need to remember that education is about broadening minds, exploring and appreciating the views of others:

> Children have a right to have their horizons extended during education at school in a way that empowers them to grow as individuals and develop their own family values.
>
> Halstead and Reiss, 2003: 115

In addition, the schooling system operates within the legal frameworks of the country including the Equality Act (2010) and a National Curriculum (DfE, 2014) which refers to that Act (including protected characteristics). Of course, schooling is just one aspect of a child's learning and development. Whether or not Relationships Education in schools is inclusive:

> Children construct their own values on the basis of all their experiences in and out of school.
>
> Halstead and Reiss, 2003: 117

This includes learning from family members and friends, the print and electronic media, and of course the social environment in which they live. When discussing Relationships Education in any setting, we need to appreciate that there will be people of faith and no faith, and a range of diversities (reflecting the protected characteristics of the Equality Act) some of which are seen and some of which are not. Whether a child is growing up in a school that has obvious diversity or not, they will live out their lives in a world filled with diversity and need to be prepared to live alongside others.

Points to consider for your setting

- How might you deal with tensions arising from the protected characteristics named in the Equality Act (2010)
- How can we enable children to develop their own viewpoints and widen their horizons?
- How does your own worldview or religious belief influence your professional role?

Key reading

- Mason, S. and Woolley, R. (2019), *Relationships and Sex Education 3 – 11: supporting children's development and well-being,* London: Bloomsbury.
- Morris, J. and Woolley, R. (eds) (2017), *Family Diversities Reading Resource,* 2nd edn, Lincoln: Bishop Grosseteste University and University of Worcester. Available online: https://libguides.bishopg.ac.uk/childrensliterature

Further reading

- Church of England (2019), *Valuing All God's Children,* 2nd edn (updated summer 2019), London: Church of England Education Office. Available online: https://www.churchofengland.org/sites/default/files/2019-07/Valuing%20All%20God%27s%20Children%20July%202019_0.pdf

References

Church of England (no date), *Church Schools and Academies.* Available online: https://www.churchofengland.org/more/education-and-schools/church-schools-and-academies (accessed 8 July 2019).

Church of England (2017), *Valuing All God's Children,* 2nd edn, London: The Church Of England Education Office.

Department for Education (DfE) (2014), *National Curriculum in England: Framework for Key Stages 1 – 4.* Available online: https://www.gov.uk/government/publications/national-curriculum-in-england-framework-for-key-stages-1-to-4/the-national-curriculum-in-england-framework-for-key-stages-1-to-4 (accessed 8 July 2019).

Department for Education (DfE) (2019), *Relationships Education, Relationships and Sex Education (RSE) and Health Education: statutory guidance for governing bodies, proprietors, head teachers, principals, senior leadership teams, teachers.* Available online: https://assets.publishing.service.gov.uk/government/uploads/system/uploads/attachment_data/file/805781/Relationships_Education__Relationships_and_Sex_Education__RSE__and_Health_Education.pdf (accessed 1 September 2019).

DfEE (2000), *Sex and Relationship Education Guidance*, Nottingham: Department for Education and Employment Publications.

Gov.uk (no date), *Faith Schools.* Available online: https://www.gov.uk/types-of-school/faith-schools (accessed 8 July 2019).

Halstead, M. and Reiss, M. (2003), *Values in Sex Education: From Principles to Practice*, London: RoutledgeFalmer.

Legislation.gov.uk (no date), *Local Government Act 1988.* Available online: http://www.legislation.gov.uk/ukpga/1988/9/contents (accessed 8 July 2019).

Morris, N. (2013), 'The return of Section 28: Schools and academies practising homophobic policy that was outlawed under Tony Blair', *Independent*, 20 August. Available online: https://www.independent.co.uk/news/uk/politics/the-return-of-section-28-schools-and-academies-practising-homophobic-policy-that-was-outlawed-under-8775249.html (accessed 8 July 2020).

Newman, L. (2011), *Donovan's Big Day,* Berkeley: Tricycle Press.

ONS (Office for National Statistics) (no date), *Religion in England and Wales 2011.* Available online: https://www.ons.gov.uk/peoplepopulationandcommunity/culturalidentity/religion/articles/religioninenglandandwales2011/2012-12-11 (accessed 8 July 2019).

Woolley, R. (2008), 'Development, well-being and attainment', in M. Cole (ed), *Professional Attributes and Practice*, 4th edn, London: David-Fulton.

Conclusion – The Future of PSHE and R(S)HE

Victoria Pugh and Daniel Hughes

We hope that after having read this book you feel more knowledgeable and ready to deliver a purposeful, effective and age-appropriate PSHE and R(S)HE curriculum whatever your setting. We encourage you to begin inspired discussions around content, delivery and possible challenges to the teaching of PSHE and R(S)HE in your setting. These discussions with colleagues, pupils, parents and the wider community offer valuable opportunities to gain a range of perspectives and assessment of needs for what needs to be taught in your particular school or setting making the curriculum bespoke and relevant.

Here is a summary of some of the key points which have been highlighted and explored within this book alongside some suggestions for future development.

- Establishing leadership for PSHE and R(S)HE is essential within a setting to ensure coverage, training opportunities, progression throughout the year groups and a common vision to support a whole-school approach. We would recommend a school-wide audit for both PSHE and R(S)HE to analyse the positive elements of your current provision and identifying any areas for development. A simple tool which can be used to support you in this is the 'Whole School Approach RSE Audit Tool' available from the Sex Education Forum website: www.sexeducationforum.org.uk
- Having a clear PSHE and separate R(S)HE policy which has had input from staff, parents, pupils and governors which is regularly updated and communicated to all.
- Remembering that high-quality PSHE and R(S)HE teaching and curriculum can make a significant contribution to learning and attainment across the curriculum.
- Regular training and update of skills are important for teachers, support staff, stakeholders and parents.

- We would recommend personal or organizational membership of the PSHE Association, available at https://www.pshe-association.org.uk/membership
- Using real life and current affairs as a springboard for discussion and an opportunity to consider our place in the wider world.
- Developing strong relationships with parents to support the work done within school is essential and opportunities for conversation and discussion with them should be encouraged.
- Regular and dedicated lesson times for PSHE and R(S)HE must be made within the daily timetable in order for lessons to be carefully planned, delivered and pupils' skills assessed. These lessons will also provide an essential space for rich discussions within a safe environment free from judgement.
- When planning and resourcing for PSHE and R(S)HE the school environment must mirror the inclusive nature of the curriculum and school ethos. This can be done through inclusive visuals around the school, use of inclusive graphics in presentations and clear understanding of vocabulary which should be used as a whole school. The policy is a great place for this vocabulary to be decided, clarified and documented to ensure consistency.
- Prepare lesson plans, supported by quality Continuing Professional Development, that respond to catastrophic incidents such as a bereavement in the school community. Having these available and ready if they are required can ease the burden and emotional challenges on staff that such situations can present.
- The examples which we have shared throughout the book highlight the importance of authentic, practical and active teaching methods and experiences for pupils. Although at time worksheets may be appropriate it can be more impactful if pupils can actively participate in group, paired and class work relating to the topics they are exploring.
- Adapting the R(S)He to meet the needs of your pupils and local community where appropriate is vital in terms of ensuring effective delivery of key content.
- It is important to remember that whilst some elements of PSHE and R(S)HE are now statutory it is likely that these are issues and topics which you have teaching within schools for a long time; do not be tempted to throw the baby out with the bath water! Keep the parts of your curriculum and practice which are already effective and engaging and add in or adapt the parts which need to be reviewed.

In addition to the importance of a separate and strong PSHE and R(S)HE curriculum, we hope this book has demonstrated how PSHE and R(S)HE can be used to enhance the whole curriculum. Remember that PSHE and R(S)HE is not just circle time!

Index